Test-Driven Development in Microsoft® .NET

James W. Newkirk
Alexei A. Vorontsov

PUBLISHED BY
Microsoft Press
A Division of Microsoft Corporation
One Microsoft Way
Redmond, Washington 98052-6399

Library of Congress Cataloging-in-Publication Data pending.

Printed and bound in the United States of America.

1 2 3 4 5 6 7 8 9   QWE   8 7 6 5 4 3

Distributed in Canada by H.B. Fenn and Company Ltd.

A CIP catalogue record for this book is available from the British Library.

Microsoft Press books are available through booksellers and distributors worldwide. For further information about international editions, contact your local Microsoft Corporation office or contact Microsoft Press International directly at fax (425) 936-7329. Visit our Web site at www.microsoft.com/learning/. Send comments to *mspinput@microsoft.com*.

Acquisitions Editors: Linda Engelman and Robin Van Steenburgh
Project Editors: Devon Musgrave and Kathleen Atkins
Indexer: Virginia Bess

Body Part No. X10-25670

This book is dedicated to my father,
William A. Newkirk

Practical wisdom is only to be learned in the school of experience. Precepts and instruction are useful so far as they go, but, without the discipline of real life, they remain of the nature of theory only — Samuel Smiles

JWN

This book is dedicated to my mother,
Larisa L. Vorontsova

A thousand-mile journey begins with the first step and can only be taken one step at a time. — An old saying

AAV

Contents at a Glance

Contents

Part III Appendixes

Foreword

I enjoyed reading this book because it stretches the boundaries of Test-Driven Development (TDD). My original TDD book demonstrated TDD in an ideal situation, in which the programmer is just typing in code and doesn't have to worry about external systems or user interfaces. After you get into the messy realities of widgets and databases, you need new techniques to continue practicing TDD and reaping its benefits, among which is confidence in cleaner code written faster.

With this book, the pieces missing from my book are included. If you want to test drive code that includes a Web interface and a database, you will learn how to do that in these pages. Even if you aren't using the Microsoft technology, you will find ideas you can carry to your application server or database.

The strength of this book is its concreteness. The extensive examples show you exactly how expert programmers use test-driven development with realistic tasks. Following the examples will show you the techniques used and, more important, the flow between the techniques. Technique can be learned from a book, but to understand the rhythm of development, you usually need to sit down with a programmer who understands it. As you read, paying careful attention to the way the techniques fit together in this book will teach you lessons about the rhythm of programming.

I think TDD is a really valuable tool. It's inexpensive, it's easy to adopt, and it brings immediate improvement. TDD has led to fewer defects, less debugging, more confidence, better design, and higher productivity in my programming practice. More important, I sleep better at night knowing that my code works in every circumstance I can think of, and I can prove it at the push of a button. This book gives you the practical advice you need to gain the benefits of TDD.

Kent Beck

Acknowledgments

We would like to thank our technical reviewers, Martin Fowler, Lee Holmes, and Eric Gunnerson. The feedback and guidance that they provided during the writing process was invaluable. In addition to the technical reviews, we also received much needed feedback and criticism from the following individuals: Charlie Poole, Paul Karsten, Peter Provost, Gregor Hohpe, Dragos Manolescu, Michael Two, Kent Beck, Ron Jeffries, Jonathan Wanagel, Scott Densmore, Naveen Yajaman, David Astels, Ward Cunningham, Benjamin Mitchell, Chris Colleran, David Trowbridge, Srinath Vasireddy, and Andrew Slocum. Their input has greatly influenced the content of the book. It is a pleasure for us to acknowledge their contributions and express our appreciation for their efforts. We would also like to thank the following people at Microsoft Press: Linda Engelman for her help getting us started and everything she did to get the book completed as soon as possible; Robin Van Steenburgh for taking over Linda's big job; Devon Musgrave for his advice on the first draft; Kathleen Atkins for her help in getting the book completed; and Nancy Sixsmith for converting what we wrote into English.

Every book is an activity that always takes more time than you think. I (James) need to thank my wife, Beth, and my children, Erin and Grant, for allowing me the time that I needed to work on the book. In fact, I owe them for all the nights and weekends that they have given up while I worked on my latest "scheme." Thank you. In addition, I would like to thank my coauthor Alexei. I thoroughly enjoyed the many hours we worked together trying to cobble together the thoughts and ideas first into a sample program and then into the text that became this book.

Writing this book took a great deal more time than can be explained, justified, or even be considered reasonable, but, without a doubt, it has been the most rewarding experience for me. I (Alexei) owe James a great deal of gratitude for giving me this opportunity. I have learned much in the process of working on the book. I would also like to thank my mentor and manager, Regan Stern, for recognizing the importance of my working on this book and supporting me in this effort.

Introduction

Many people think that Test-Driven Development (TDD) is all about testing software. In fact, test-driven development's main goal is not testing software, but aiding the programmer and customer during the development process with unambiguous requirements. The requirements are expressed in the form of tests, which are a support mechanism (scaffolding, you might say) that stands firmly under the participants as they undertake the hazards of software development. However, that is not the only purpose of testing. As you will see, the tests, once written, are valuable resources in their own right.

What Are the Benefits of Using Tests?

It is important during development that problems are discovered early and corrected when they are found. Often, the biggest problems occur when there is a misunderstanding of a requirement between the consumers of the software (customers) and the producers (programmers). These types of problems could be avoided if there were a way to specify these requirements unambiguously before development begins. Enter tests. The tests specify requirements in a way that does not require human interpretation to indicate success or failure. If there is a sufficient number of tests and they are present prior to development, simply running the tests and indicating success or failure helps solve the old problem of software development, "Are We Done?" The answer is no longer an interpretation; the code either passes all the tests or it does not. After it passes, it's done.

Solving this problem alone may be justification enough, but is there more? The tests that are written during development can be run and enhanced by Quality Assurance (QA) with tests of their own. Due to the code being written with testing as a primary motivation, the resulting code should be easier to test. Having a base of existing tests and code that is easier to test should allow QA to shift from a reactive mode into a more proactive mode.

The tests themselves are useful not only in the initial development of the software; if they are maintained along with the production code, they can be used in the ongoing development of the software. For example, if a problem is discovered in the production code, the first step should be to write a test to clearly identify the problem and then, after you have a failing test, correct the problem. This new test specifies a scenario that was not identified during the prior development. If you do this consistently, the tests will evolve into how the program is used in real life, which increases their value exponentially. When adding new features, you could run this suite of tests to ensure that the new code does not break any of the existing tests. If the test coverage is sufficient; running the tests and getting a successful result should reduce your fear of moving forward. Fear of breaking existing functionality can cause you to become overly cautious, which slows you down. Think of the tests as a way of covering your back.

An Example

Let's look at an example to demonstrate how tests can describe a requirement more clearly than words can. Consider the following description of a Stack. "A *Stack* is a data structure in which you can access only the item at the top. With a computer, *Stack* just like a stack of dishes—you add items to the top and remove them from the top" (*http://www.developersdomain.com/vb/articles/ stack.htm*). This is not a bad description, but it does not specify method names and it uses an analogy that might not resonate with people. In short, it leaves a great deal open to interpretation, and you would get many implementations that could satisfy this definition.

Now look at a test that specifies the same thing:

```
[Test]
public void PushPop()
{
    string name = "Name";
    Stack stack = new Stack();
    stack.Push(name);
    Assert.AreEqual(name, stack.Pop());
}
```

This code specifies the names of methods, how they are called, and what they should return. It also specifies a sequence that yields a successful result. Finally, the test is executable, meaning that you can run it on the production code, and it will inform you if your implementation passes the test. The only thing that is open to interpretation is how you should implement the *Stack*, which is exactly what you want if you are a programmer. If your job was to implement a *Stack*, would you rather have your specification described as a series of tests or as a written specification?

Organization

This book is organized into two sections, followed by three appendixes.

- **Part I: Test-Driven Development Overview** This section describes the concepts of test-driven development. It begins with Kent Beck's rules, provides some additional detail about how to use and apply these rules, defines terminology that we use throughout the book, and defines a process for doing test-driven development. In addition to the definitions, we also demonstrate how to apply them by example. The focus in these early chapters is on completeness and following the principles and practices as written.

- **Part II: The Test-Driven Development Example** This section demonstrates how to do Test-Driven Development on a realistic *n*-tier application. The application, a media library, is specified in Chapter 4, "The Media Library Example." As well as implementing the expected functionality, we also investigate important real-world application areas that are typically avoided in sample applications. For example, we demonstrate the use of TDD with concepts such as exception handling and database connectivity. By the end of the sample, you'll have a good grounding in the techniques needed to use TDD in your own enterprise projects.

- **Appendix A: NUnit Primer** This appendix contains an introduction to the tool, NUnit.

- **Appendix B: Transactions in ADO.NET** This appendix provides an overview of transaction support in the .NET Framework.

- **Appendix C: Bibliography** The bibliography lists the works by other people that we have used ourselves and referred readers to throughout this book.

How to Use This Book

This book is written primarily for experienced programmers. You will get more value from this book if you are familiar with C# syntax and understand object-oriented programming. However, even if your primary development language is not C#, you should be able to port the example to other .NET languages, such as Microsoft Visual Basic .NET. The more complicated concepts do have overview material and pointers to additional sources of information.

If You Have Never Used NUnit Before

Read Chapter 1, "Test-Driven Development Practices." Then read Appendix A, "NUnit Primer," which describes the tool that is used for technology facing or programmer tests in the text. Then you can proceed with the rest of the content.

If You Are a Manager or Business Analyst

Read Chapter 1, which introduces the concepts and the process. Then read Chapter 7, "Customer Tests: Completing the First Feature," in which we discuss ways to use tests without having to write them in C#. We use a tool named FIT (*http://fit.c2.com*) to implement the business-facing or customer tests.

Small Steps—A Personal Story

Sometimes, people ask me (James) how I got started doing test-driven development. I want to relate this story because as a result of this experience, I finally believed that a series of small steps, verified each time by tests, could actually lead to a better solution. Up until this point, I knew the rules but not how to apply them.

It was December of 1999. I was at Object Mentor, and we were in the midst of the first XP immersion class. Kent Beck, Ron Jeffries, Martin Fowler, Robert C. Martin, Michael Hill, Fred George, Alan Francis, and others were my companions. Needless to say, it was an incredible week, not so much from the perspective of a class, but from being around such an awesome array of talent all focused on this thing called Extreme Programming. Besides participating in the class, I was working on a new Java class that I would be presenting the following January. I was trying to incorporate aspects of refactoring and test-first programming using JUnit (*http://www.junit.org*) into the class. My thought was to write an awful program and then use it to teach the concepts of refactoring. (That same awful program, implemented in C#, is the basis for Chapter 3, "Refactoring—By Example.")

I was working alone, and the staging of the example was not working well because it turns out that my refactoring steps were much too large. Kent came over and asked what I was doing after noticing me working on code by myself; I told him that I was trying to work out an example of refactoring for my upcoming class. After looking at what I did, he told me he thought I should start over. Instead of walking away, he offered to sit down and help me. During the next hour or so, the whole idea of the small incremental changes leading to a better solution became a reality. This awful code was transformed into something that was very clear and easily understandable.

It is only after I spent that time working with Kent directly that I began to understand just how small the steps were that Kent, Ron, and Martin were talking about. In fact, we thought that this in itself would be a useful activity for the whole class to see the following day. So, Robert Martin went home that night and constructed some UML diagrams around the code and came up with a slightly different implementation of the same algorithm that Kent and I refactored in front of the class the next day. For a couple of hours, we walked step-by-step through the code—making the smallest of changes and then running the tests to make sure that we did not break anything. When we were finished, someone said that we had made 40 separate changes to the code. The code was so much clearer that it was remarkable. Alexei and I have used the same problem that taught me so much during the class as the sample in Chapter 3 so that you can also benefit from that experience.

Companion Web Site

Many of the code samples in this book were too long to print without interruption by explanatory text. If you prefer to see the complete code samples from the early chapters and the sample application in its entirety, you can go to *http://workspaces.gotdotnet.com/tdd*.

Part I

Test-Driven Development Primer

1

Test-Driven Development Practices

In this chapter, we define test-driven development (TDD) and then describe a process for applying it when developing software.

What Is Test-Driven Development?

Kent Beck, in his book *Test-Driven Development: By Example* (Addison-Wesley Professional, 2003), defines test-driven development using the following rules:

- Never write a single line of code unless you have a failing automated test.

- Eliminate duplication.

The first rule is straightforward: don't write code without having a failing automated test because the tests embody the requirements that the code must satisfy, as stated in the Introduction. If there is no requirement (that is, test), there is no need to implement anything. This rule prevents us from implementing functionality that is not tested and not needed in the solution.

The second rule states that no code should be duplicated in the program. Code duplication is the epitome of bad software design; it leads to inconsistency problems and a reduced level of confidence in the program over time as people forget where the duplications are. If there is code duplication, it is the programmer's job to remove it when it is seen. (In Extreme Programming [XP], this rule is called "Once and Only Once!")

Test Types

Kent's definition does not make a distinction between different types of tests.[1] All he says is that the tests have to be automated, which we agree with entirely. However, it is useful to categorize the test types around the constituents who produce them—for example, customers who specify the functionality, programmers who implement the functionality, and testers who support development during the development of the code and critique the final result after the code is complete. The two constituents that this book focuses on are programmers and customers.

> **More Info**   For information about testers, see Brian Marick's website (*http://www.testing.com*).

Programmer Tests

If we are talking about the programmers writing the code, it is useful to think of these tests as focused on technology, so you can refer to them as *technology facing* or *programmer tests*. Some people refer to this type of test as a *unit test*; we are specifically not calling it that because unit testing's purpose is much different from what we are doing in TDD. Because the audience for these tests is programmers, it is critically important that the tests be written in a language that the programmers understand. (It's even better if they are in the same language as the production code.) If the tests are in the same language, the programmer doesn't have to change paradigms to write tests. The programmer tests in this book are written in C# and are run in a tool named NUnit (*http://www.nunit.org*).

Customer Tests

Tests that customers use to specify the functionality they need and how it should work can be referred to as *business facing* or *customer tests*. These types of tests are often referred to as *acceptance tests* or *functional tests*. As in the case of programmer tests, the tests need to be written in a language that the customer understands. The goal is to empower the customer to be able to write tests. The customer tests in this book are written using a tool named Framework for Integrated Test (FIT) (*http://fit.c2.com*).

---

1. The categorization that we present here comes from Brian Marick (*http://www.testing.com*). Brian has written about the role of testers on Agile projects and TDD in general. We encourage you to visit his website.

Simple Design

"Simplicity is more complicated than you think. But it's well worth it" (Ron Jeffries et al., *Extreme Programming Installed*, Addison-Wesley, 2001).

In a previous section, TDD was defined as a couple of rules. However, that definition leaves out a practice that is implied by the rules but not stated explicitly. Because the tests define the requirements, your job when writing the code should be to satisy the requirements *no less* and *no more*. Everyone understands *no less* (the program would not work otherwise), but not everyone understands *no more*.

What is meant by *no more*? Think back to a time when someone asked you to add a feature to an existing system, and you said "No problem; I thought this was going to happen and put additional code in for this specific purpose." You were viewed as a hero because you anticipated the requirement and had already implemented the solution.

Now remember a time when you added complexity in the form of additional functions, abstract classes, and so on that nobody ever asked for. This additional code has to be maintained along with the rest of the useful software. In fact, the maintenance burden of this software is worse because it is not supported by real usage. So you should always strive to do *no more* and *no less*, as follows:

- The code is appropriate for the intended audience.

- The code passes all the tests.

- The code communicates everything it needs to.

- The code has the smallest number of classes.

- The code has the smallest number of methods.

The highest priority is that the code be appropriate for the audience. For example, if you are writing a parser for youself to read, you would likely use a generator because you are the person reading the code. If you were writing a parser for someone new to parsing, you might use a parsing technique called recursive descent to better illustrate how parsing works. Either approach is suitable; you just need to keep in mind who the audience for your solution is. After you have satisfied the appropriateness requirement, the next-highest priority is that the code must pass all the tests. When all the tests pass, the code has to communicate the intent as clearly as possible. (Code can be duplicated if the purpose is to better communicate the design intent.) The last two criteria state that the implementation should have the smallest number of classes and methods after the first three criteria are satisfied.

You might think that achieving simplicity is an easy process. Think again—it's often very difficult. However, the simpler the code is, the more resilient it is and the easier it is to modify.

Refactoring

Refactoring is defined as improving the code while not changing its functionality. The definitive book on refactoring is Martin Fowler's, *Refactoring: Improving the Design of Existing Code* (Addison-Wesley, 1999). This is a book you should own and read cover to cover. (Even though the examples are in Java, the concepts presented transcend the language.)

Refactoring is a critical part of TDD because you need to refine the code's design as you add additional tests. For example, if you see duplicated code in the solution, you need to remove it. If you need to introduce complexity to remove the duplication, it is all right because there is an actual need, not an anticipated need. Following this practice diligently yields an implementation that is complex where it needs to be; no more and no less. It is through refactoring and simple design that you can refine the system's design to meet the requirements specified by the tests.

> **More Info**   See Chapter 3, "Refactoring—By Example," for a step-by-step demonstration of refactoring.

Process

In the previous section, we defined TDD, simple design, and refactoring. In this section we define a process that can be used to do TDD. There are two aspects to the process: One aspect is focused at a task or feature level, and the other focuses on an individual test.

Test List

In Kent Beck's book, *Test-Driven Development: By Example* (Addison-Wesley, 2003), he describes a *test list*. When starting a new task or feature, you need to brainstorm a list of tests. As you think about these tests, write them down. In addition to describing the requirements unambiguously, this *test list* also indicates the scope of the activity and is the most complete definition of the completion criteria. How long should you spend doing this? For most tasks that end up taking about 4 hours, we spend about 15–20 minutes doing this activity. If the scope of the list is too large, the list can be the basis for further estimation.

After the list is complete, you need to choose the first test to implement. The main criterion is that the test you pick should provide useful feedback for the problem that you are solving. As you complete each test, just cross it off the list. When there are no more tests left to implement, you are finished. See Chapter 2, "Test-Driven Development in .NET—By Example" for an example of a *test list* for the implementation of the *Stack*.

Red/Green/Refactor

Red/Green/Refactor defines the process for implementing each test in the test list. The goal of this process is to work in small, verifiable steps that provide immediate feedback. William Wake, in his book *Extreme Programming Explored* (Addison-Wesley, 2001), details the programming tasks as follows:

1.   Write the test code.

2.   Compile the test code.

     (It should fail because you haven't implemented anything yet.)

3.   Implement just enough to compile.

4.   Run the test and see it fail.

5.   Implement just enough to make the test pass.

6.   Run the test and see it pass.

7.   Refactor for clarity and to eliminate duplication.

8.   Repeat from the top.

If followed literally, this process forces you to work in very small steps—so small that at first you may think that individually they are ridiculous. However, the smaller the step, the easier it is to determine whether you made a mistake. The alternative is to wait until you have made a lot of changes to the code and then run the tests. If something fails after you have made a lot of changes to the code, you don't know which change was the one that caused the failure. In fact, if you can work in really small steps with the tests providing immediate feedback, you can forget about using the debugger; you'll know exactly where to look because the step was so small. Working in small, verifiable steps increases your speed in moving forward because you will be moving with more confidence; this confidence is the result of feedback that running the tests provides you.

Summary

In this chapter, we defined the terminology and practices that make up test-driven development. We described a process you follow to implement each individual test. In the next chapter, we use this process on a well-known problem to allow you to focus on the process instead of the problem.

2

Test-Driven Development in .NET—By Example

In this chapter, we'll demonstrate how to implement a *Stack* using Test-Driven Development (TDD). We have found that the best way to understand TDD is to see it practiced and follow along step by step. The following are the steps we used to build a *Stack* using this method.

The Task

The task is to implement an unbounded *Stack*, which is a data structure in which access is restricted to the most recently inserted item.

> **Note** An *unbounded Stack* doesn't have to be presized, and you can insert an unlimited number of elements onto it.

The operations include *Push, Pop, Top,* and *IsEmpty.* The *Push* function inserts an element onto the top of the *Stack.* The *Pop* function removes the topmost element and returns it; the *Top* operation returns the topmost element but does not remove it from the *Stack.* The *IsEmpty* function returns true when there are no elements on the *Stack.* Figure 2-1 shows the *Push* operation in action, Figure 2-2 shows the *Pop* operation, and Figure 2-3 shows the *Top* operation.

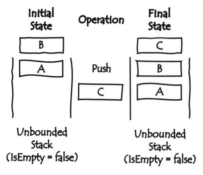

Figure 2-1   *Push* operation

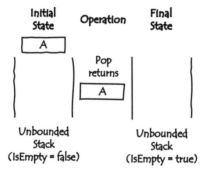

Figure 2-2   *Pop* operation

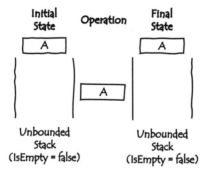

Figure 2-3   *Top* operation

Test List[1]

In Chapter 1, "Test-Driven Development Practices," we stated that the first step is to brainstorm a list of tests for the task. The goal of this activity is to create a

---

1. Beck, Kent. *Test-Driven Development: By Example.* Addison-Wesley, 2003.

test list that verifies the detailed requirements and describes the completion criteria. One thing to keep in mind is that the list is not static. As you implement each test, you might have to revisit the list to add new tests or delete them as appropriate.

Let's try to write the test list for the unbounded *Stack*.

Unbounded *Stack* Test List

- Create a *Stack* and verify that *IsEmpty* is true.

- *Push* a single object on the *Stack* and verify that *IsEmpty* is false.

- *Push* a single object, *Pop* the object, and verify that *IsEmpty* is true.

- *Push* a single object, remembering what it is; *Pop* the object, and verify that the two objects are equal.

- *Push* three objects, remembering what they are; *Pop* each one, and verify that they are removed in the correct order.

- *Pop* a *Stack* that has no elements.

- *Push* a single object and then call *Top*. Verify that *IsEmpty* is false.

- *Push* a single object, remembering what it is; and then call *Top*. Verify that the object that is returned is the same as the one that was pushed.

- Call *Top* on a *Stack* with no elements.

Choosing the First Test

There are differing opinions about which test to choose first. One says that you should choose the simplest test that gets you started and solves a small piece of the problem. Another says that you should choose a test that describes the essence of what you are trying to accomplish. For example, looking at the test list in the previous section, the simplest test is the first one: Create an empty *Stack* and verify that *IsEmpty* is true. This operation looks as if it would be easy to implement, but it does not provide a great deal of useful feedback when developing a *Stack* because the *IsEmpty* function is a supporting function.

A test in the list that is closer to the essence of the problem is the following: *Push* a single object, remembering what it is; *Pop* the object, and verify that it is equal to the object that was pushed. In this test, you are verifying that the *Push* and *Pop* methods work as expected. Which style to use really is a matter of personal preference because both will work.

There are times when the essence approach can take too much time to implement. If that is the case, you should choose a simpler test to get started. The suggestion that we give people who are learning TDD is to choose the simplest test approach and graduate to the essence approach after becoming familiar with the technique. Therefore, the first test that we chose to implement is "Create an empty *Stack* and verify that *IsEmpty* is true."

Red/Green/Refactor

The following is the implementation of each test in the test list.

Test 1: Create a *Stack* and verify that *IsEmpty* is true.

This test requires creating a *Stack* and then calling the *IsEmpty* property. The *IsEmpty* property should return true because we haven't put any elements into the *Stack*. Let's create a file called StackFixture.cs, in which we write a test fixture class, called *StackFixture*, to hold the tests.

```
using System;
using NUnit.Framework;

[TestFixture]
public class StackFixture
{ /* … */ }
```

There are a few things of interest about this class. The line *using NUnit.Framework;* is needed to reference the custom attributes defined in NUnit that are used to mark the test fixture. The *[TestFixture]* attribute can be associated only with a class. This attribute is an indicator to NUnit that the class contains test methods.

The next activity is to write the method that does the test. (Here, the test method name is *Empty*.)

```
[Test]
public void Empty()
{
    Stack stack = new Stack();
    Assert.IsTrue(stack.IsEmpty);
}
```

The test method is marked with the attribute *[Test]*. The first thing is to create a *Stack* object. After creating the object, we use the *Assert.IsTrue(…)* method to verify that the return value of *IsEmpty* is true.

Although the class used in the test, *Stack*, and the property *IsEmpty* do not exist, we are writing test code as if they do. We are thinking about how the class and its methods are used instead of how to implement it, which is an important distinction. This is why many people refer to test-driven development as much a design technique as a testing technique. Many times, class library designers implement a library and then figure out how to use it, which can lead to libraries that require a lot of initialization, complex method interactions, and increased dependencies. Thinking about how to use the library before implementing it places a greater emphasis on usage, which often leads to better design.

Because the *Stack* class does not exist, the test does not compile. That's easy enough to fix. What is the smallest amount of work that needs to be done to get this to compile?

```
using System;

public class Stack
{
    private bool isEmpty = true;

    public bool IsEmpty
    {
        get
        {
            return isEmpty;
        }
    }
}
```

This implementation is certainly small; in fact, it might seem surprising. Remember that the goal is to do the smallest amount of work possible to get the code to compile. Some people might say that this code is too complicated: given the test, they might argue that the following code would be sufficient:

```
public bool IsEmpty
{
    get
    {
        return true;
    }
}
```

There is a balance to achieve between anticipating future tests and implementation and being totally ignorant of the next test. In the beginning, you should focus on the test you are writing and not think about the other tests. As you become familiar with the technique and the task, you can increase the size of the steps. You should always keep in mind that large steps are harder to debug than smaller steps. Also, if your code is too complicated or provides functionality that is not tested, additional refactorings can result later.

This discussion is also relevant to the earlier discussion about the test list. It is very clear from the test list that you have to store multiple items. Should you go ahead and use an *ArrayList* because you might need it later? No—the current tests do not support the need for an *ArrayList*. Wait and see what the tests look like before making that decision.

Now that the code compiles, it is time to run the test in NUnit. The green bar displays, which indicates success. We can check off the first test and move on.

Which test should we choose next? Perhaps we should stay focused on the *IsEmpty* property because it is probably the smallest increment over what we have now. Let's look at "*Push* a single object on the *Stack* and verify that *IsEmpty* is false."

Test 2: *Push* a single object on the *Stack* and verify that *IsEmpty* is false.

Test 2 says to *Push* an object onto the *Stack* and then verify that *IsEmpty* returns false. Let's try and write a test that does this. We'll call the method *PushOne*:

```
[Test]
public void PushOne()
{
    Stack stack = new Stack();
    stack.Push("first element");
    Assert.IsFalse(stack.IsEmpty,
      "After Push, IsEmpty should be false");
}
```

The test, like the previous one, creates a *Stack* object. Then, using a method named *Push* puts a *String* object onto the *Stack*. Finally, we call the *IsEmpty* property on *Stack* and verify that it returns false.

Of course, this code does not compile because we have not defined the *Push* method. Once again, what is the minimal amount of work needed to get this code to compile?

```
public void Push(object element)
{
}
```

That is as small as it gets. Now, we can run the test. Running the tests yields the following result:

```
Tests run: 2, Failures: 1, Not run: 0, Time: 0.015627 seconds

Failures:
1) StackFixture.PushOne : After Push, IsEmpty should be false
    at StackFixture.PushOne() in c:\stackfixture.cs:line 19
```

The test failed because it was expecting the *IsEmpty* property of the *Stack* to return false and it returned true. Now that we have a failing test, we can implement *Push* correctly. Clearly, we need to change the *isEmpty* member variable to be false when an element is pushed onto the *Stack*. The *Push* method also implies that we have to store the elements in some collection to satisfy the other operations, but there are no tests for this, so we will wait until we have tests to implement this behavior. Let's change the *Push* method to implement this correctly.

```
public void Push(object element)
{
    isEmpty = false;
}
```

Before we decide which test to implement next, we need to make sure that there is no code duplication. The *StackFixture* class has some duplicated test code. The test code is just as important as the production code; it is critical to the overall communication and it also serves as an example of how the client code should work. Both the *PushOne* and *Empty* tests create a *Stack* in the first line of their methods. So, let's move the creation of the *Stack* object from the test methods to a new method called *Init*. After the modifications are completed, the *StackFixture* class looks like this:

```
using System;
using NUnit.Framework;

[TestFixture]
public class StackFixture
{
    private Stack stack;

    [SetUp]
    public void Init()
    {
        stack = new Stack();
    }

    [Test]
    public void Empty()
```

```
    {
        Assert.IsTrue(stack.IsEmpty);
    }

    [Test]
    public void PushOne()
    {
        stack.Push("first element");
        Assert.IsFalse(stack.IsEmpty,
            "After Push, IsEmpty should be false");
    }
}
```

We had to create a private instance variable called *stack* so that all the methods of the class could access the same object. The function *Init* is marked with an attribute called [*SetUp*]. NUnit uses this attribute to ensure that this method is called prior to each test being run, which means that each test method gets a newly created *Stack*, instead of one modified from a previous test.

This is an excellent example of the second rule of TDD: eliminate duplication. Prior to the refactoring, there was a small amount of duplicated code in *StackFixture*. It may seem trivial, but it serves as an example of how following red/green/refactor leads to code that is cleaner and easier to understand. It also has the added benefit of making the tests easier to maintain because changes to the initialization code would be made in one place.

Because the code compiled and passed the tests, it's time to move on to the next test. We want to stay focused on the *IsEmpty* property, so *Push* a single object, *Pop* the object and verify that *IsEmpty* is true seems like a natural.

Test 3: *Push* a single object, *Pop* the object, and verify that *IsEmpty* is true.

This test introduces a new method called *Pop*, which returns the topmost element and removes it from the *Stack*. To test that behavior, we need to insert an element onto the *Stack* and then remove it. After that sequence is completed, calling *IsEmpty* on the *Stack* should be true. Let's see what that test looks like:

```
    [Test]
    public void Pop()
    {
        stack.Push("first element");
        stack.Pop();
        Assert.IsTrue(stack.IsEmpty,
            "After Push - Pop, IsEmpty should be true");
    }
```

Of course, the code does not compile because we haven't defined the method *Pop*. So we'll fake it:[2]

```
public void Pop()
{
}
```

The code compiles, but the tests fail with the following message:

```
Tests run: 3, Failures: 1, Not run: 0, Time: 0.0156336 seconds

Failures:
1) StackFixture.Pop : After Push - Pop, IsEmpty should be true
   at StackFixture.Pop() in c:\stackfixture.cs:line 33
```

We now need to implement the *Pop* method so that it passes the test. We will simply change *IsEmpty* to be true when *Pop* is called.

```
public void Pop()
{
    isEmpty = true;
}
```

The code compiles and we run the tests. The tests pass, so we can check off Test 3 on the test list.

Notice that the implemented *Pop* method returns *void*. The requirements stated previously said that *Pop* should also return the topmost element. Because we do not have a test that tests that functionality, we will leave it that way until we have a failing test.

So far, we have been concerned with verifying that the *IsEmpty* property on the *Stack* is correct in regard to the *Push* and *Pop* operations. However, this is leading to code that does not further our understanding of the problem. In fact, we have written three tests that manage a Boolean variable. It is now time to change direction and look at the actual objects that are pushed and popped onto the *Stack*.

Test 4: *Push* a single object, remembering what it is; *Pop* the object, and verify that the two objects are equal.

In this test, we need to create an object (in this case, an *int*), push the object onto the *Stack*, pop the *Stack*, and verify that the object that is returned is equal to the object pushed on the *Stack*. The following is the test method *PushPop-ContentCheck*:

---

2. Beck, Kent. *Test-Driven Development: By Example*. Addison-Wesley, 2003.

```
[Test]
public void PushPopContentCheck()
{
    int expected = 1234;
    stack.Push(expected);
    int actual = (int)stack.Pop();
    Assert.AreEqual(expected, actual);
}
```

Of course, this code does not compile. The *Pop* method returns *void*, not *object*. So let's change the *Pop* method to return an *object*. The simplest code is to have it return *null*:

```
public object Pop()
{
    isEmpty = true;
    return null;
}
```

Let's compile and run the tests. The code compiles, but the tests fail with the following message:

```
Tests run: 4, Failures: 1, Not run: 0, Time: 0.0156311 seconds

Failures:

1) StackFixture.PushPopContentCheck : System.NullReferenceException : Object
reference not set to an instance of an object.
   at StackFixture.PushPopContentCheck() in c:\stackfixture.cs:line 42
```

The test failed because we did not return the value that was on the top of the *Stack*. In order for this test to pass, we have to change the *Push* method to retain the object and alter the *Pop* method to return the object. The following code is our next attempt:

```
using System;

public class Stack
{
    private bool isEmpty = true;
    private object element;

    public bool IsEmpty
    {
        get
        {
            return isEmpty;
        }
    }
```

```
public void Push(object element)
{
    this.element = element;
    isEmpty = false;
}

public object Pop()
{
    isEmpty = true;
    object top = element;
    element = null;

    return top;
}
}
```

Let's compile and run the tests. All the tests pass, so we can now mark this test off the list. Before we move on, let's do a little refactoring because there is a change that could be made related to the *isEmpty* member variable. The change that we will make is to remove the *isEmpty* member variable and replace it with a conditional expression using the *element* member variable. Here is the modified code for the *Stack*:

```
using System;

public class Stack
{
    private object element;

    public bool IsEmpty
    {
        get
        {
            return (element == null);
        }
    }

    public void Push(object element)
    {
        this.element = element;
    }

    public object Pop()
    {
        object top = element;
        element = null;

        return top;
    }
}
```

This is much better because we use the *element* variable itself to represent whether the *Stack* is empty or not. Prior to this, we had to update two variables; now we use only one variable, which makes this solution better and we can move on. One of the key behaviors of the *Stack* is that when you push an element onto the *Stack,* it becomes the topmost element. Therefore, if you push more than one item, the *Stack* should push the top item down and replace the top item with the newly pushed item. This behavior should be consistent, no matter how many items have been pushed.

We want the next test to verify that the *Stack* works as expected.

Test 5: *Push* three objects, remembering what they are; *Pop* each one, and verify that they are correct.

The previous test, *PushPopContentCheck*, pushed and popped only one item. In this test, we have to push three items to ensure that the *Stack* behaves in the correct fashion:

```
[Test]
public void PushPopMultipleElements()
{
    string pushed1 = "1";
    stack.Push(pushed1);
    string pushed2 = "2";
    stack.Push(pushed2);
    string pushed3 = "3";
    stack.Push(pushed3);

    string popped = (string)stack.Pop();
    Assert.AreEqual(pushed3, popped);
    popped = (string)stack.Pop();
    Assert.AreEqual(pushed2, popped);
    popped = (string)stack.Pop();
    Assert.AreEqual(pushed1, popped);
}
```

In the *PushPopMultipleElements* method, we push 3 items onto the *Stack* and then pop them off and verify that they are in the correct order. In this example, we push *"1"*, *"2"*, and *"3"* in that order and verify that when we call *Pop* repeatedly, the strings come off *"3"*, *"2"*, and *"1"*.

Let's compile and run the tests. The code compiles, but NUnit fails with the following message:

```
Tests run: 5, Failures: 1, Not run: 0, Time: 0.031238 seconds

Failures:
```

```
1) StackFixture.PushPopMultipleElements :
       expected:<"2">
         but was:<(null)>
    at StackFixture.PushPopMultipleElements() in c:\stackfixture.cs:line 59
```

Clearly, something is wrong. In fact, we can no longer use the simplistic implementation of the *Stack* with a single element. We need to use a collection to hold the elements inside the *Stack*. After making a series of changes, here is the refactored *Stack* code:

```csharp
using System;
using System.Collections;

public class Stack
{
    private ArrayList elements = new ArrayList();

    public bool IsEmpty
    {
        get
        {
            return (elements.Count == 0);
        }
    }

    public void Push(object element)
    {
        elements.Insert(0, element);
    }

    public object Pop()
    {
        object top = elements[0];
        elements.RemoveAt(0);
        return top;
    }
}
```

Let's compile and run the tests. The code compiles and all the tests pass, so we can move on. You should notice that we made big changes to the entire implementation, and no tests were broken afterward. This is a good example of building confidence in the code that we have tests for. We are assured that, based on our tests, the code is no worse than it was previously (which is the best the tests can demonstrate).

This example shows very well the benefits of delaying implementation decisions while writing tests. Some would argue that we should have started out using an *ArrayList* to hold the elements of the *Stack* because it was a foregone conclusion that we would need a collection to hold the elements. We did not do this because we are trying to let the tests drive the need for functionality instead of us thinking we know what is needed and then writing tests that verify that thinking. It is a difference that this test demonstrates very clearly.

So far, we have been careful to call *Pop* on a *Stack* only when it contains elements. In the next test, we need to look at what happens when we call *Pop* on a *Stack* that has no elements.

Test 6: *Pop* a *Stack* that has no elements.

What should happen if we call *Pop* on the *Stack* and there are no elements? There are a number of options:

■   We could return *null* for the value (although we could never store *null* on the *Stack*).

■   We could use an in/out parameter to indicate success or failure of the *Pop* operation. This procedure is clumsy and requires the user to check the value to determine whether the method was successful.

■   We could throw an exception because it's an error we don't expect to occur.

Reviewing the options, it seems to make the most sense to have the *Pop* method throw an exception if there are no elements on the *Stack*. Let's write a test that expects the *Pop* operation to throw an exception:

```
[Test]
[ExpectedException(typeof(InvalidOperationException))]
public void PopEmptyStack()
{
    stack.Pop();
}
```

This test uses another attribute in NUnit that allows the programmer to declare that the execution of the test is expected to throw an exception. We could define a new exception, but we choose to use *InvalidOperationException* in this example. It is in the *System* namespace and is defined as "The exception that is thrown when a method call is invalid for the object's current state."[3]

We compiled and ran the tests. The test failed with the following message:

---

3. .NET SDK Documentation, System.InvalidOperationException

```
Tests run: 6, Failures: 1, Not run: 0, Time: 0.0156248 seconds
```

```
Failures:
1) StackFixture.PopEmptyStack : Expected: InvalidOperationException but was Arg
umentOutOfRangeException
    at System.Collections.ArrayList.get_Item(Int32 index)
    at Stack.Pop() in c:\projects\book\stack\stack.cs:line 23
    at StackFixture.PopEmptyStack() in c:\stackfixture.cs:line 68
```

Not surprisingly, it does not work; we never changed the *Pop* method to return the exception. However, we did get an exception, just not the right one. The *ArgumentOutOfRangeException* occurs when you access an array outside of the allowable range of values. In this case, there were no elements in the array. Clearly, we need to modify the *Pop* method to check to see whether there are any elements in the *Stack* and if not, throw the *InvalidOperationException*. Let's modify the *Pop* method to throw the correct exception:

```
public object Pop()
{
    if(IsEmpty) throw new
            InvalidOperationException("cannot pop an empty stack");

    object top = elements[0];
    elements.RemoveAt(0);
    return top;
}
```

That works. We can now check this test off the list and figure out which test to do next.

As we were implementing this test, a few additional tests came to mind, so we need to add them to our *test list*. We want to add tests to verify that the *Stack* works when the arguments are equal to *null*. The new tests are as follows:

- *Push null* onto the *Stack* and verify that *IsEmpty* returns false.

- *Push null* onto the *Stack*, *Pop* the *Stack*, and verify that the value returned is *null*.

- *Push null* onto the *Stack*, call *Top*, and verify that the value returned is *null*.

Reviewing the test list indicates that we have not done anything yet with the *Top* method, so let's focus on that next.

Test 7: *Push* a single object and then call *Top*. Verify that *IsEmpty* returns false.

The *Top* method does not change the state of the *Stack*; it simply returns the topmost element. This test verifies that *IsEmpty* is not affected by the call to *Top*. Let's write that test:

```
[Test]
public void PushTop()
{
    stack.Push("42");
    stack.Top();
    Assert.IsFalse(stack.IsEmpty);
}
```

Of course, this code does not compile. We have not written the *Top* method, so we'll fake it:

```
public object Top()
{
    return null;
}
```

That works. So we'll check off another item on the list and decide which test to implement next.

Not so fast! There are a couple of tests that we need to add to the test list that we thought of while doing this test.

■ *Push* multiple items onto the *Stack* and verify that calling *Top* returns the correct object.

■ *Push* an item on the *Stack*, call *Top* repeatedly, and verify that the object returned each time is equal to the object that was pushed onto the *Stack*.

The test list now contains 14 items. These last two tests are important because they verify that *Top* works as expected. We didn't think of them at the beginning, but they came to mind when we started working on *Top*.

The next test we will implement verifies that *Top* returns the correct object.

Test 8: *Push* a single object, remembering what it is; and then call *Top*. Verify that the object that is returned is equal to the one that was pushed.

In the previous test, we checked to see whether the *IsEmpty* property was correct after we called *Top*. In this test, we verify that the object pushed onto the *Stack* is equal to the one we get back when we call *Top*:

```
[Test]
public void PushTopContentCheckOneElement()
{
    string pushed = "42";
    stack.Push(pushed);
    string topped = (string)stack.Top();
    Assert.Equals(pushed, topped);
}
```

Let's compile and run the tests. NUnit protests with the following message:

```
Tests run: 8, Failures: 1, Not run: 0, Time: 0.0312442 seconds


Failures:
1) StackFixture.PushTopContentCheckOneElement :
        expected:<"42">
          but was:<(null)>
    at StackFixture.PushTopContentCheckOneElement()
      in c:\stackfixture.cs:line 84
```

In the previous test, we faked the implementation of *Top* by just returning *null*. Looks like we have to implement (make) it correctly for this test to pass:

```
public object Top()
{
    return elements[0];
}
```

That works. Although *Top* seems similar to *Pop*, let's wait and see whether it gets more obvious as we add additional tests. Let's write another test.

Test 9: *Push* multiple objects, remembering what they are; call *Top*, and verify that the last item pushed is equal to the one returned by *Top*.

This test states that we need to push more than one object onto the *Stack* and then call *Top*. The return value of *Top* should be equal to the last value that was pushed onto the *Stack*. Let's give it a try:

```
[Test]
public void PushTopContentCheckMultiples()
{
    string pushed3 = "3";
    stack.Push(pushed3);
    string pushed4 = "4";
    stack.Push(pushed4);
    string pushed5 = "5";
    stack.Push(pushed5);

    string topped = (string)stack.Top();
    Assert.AreEqual(pushed5, topped);
}
```

That works. This one just happens to work, so good for us. The next test verifies that calling *Top* repeatedly always returns the same object.

Test 10: *Push* one object and call *Top* repeatedly, comparing what is returned to what was pushed.

As stated previously, the *Top* method is not supposed to change the state of the object, so we should be able to push an object onto the *Stack* and then call *Top* as many times as we want—and it should always return the same object. Let's code it and see whether it works:

```
[Test]
public void PushTopNoStackStateChange()
{
    string pushed = "44";
    stack.Push(pushed);

    for(int index = 0; index < 10; index++)
    {
        string topped = (string)stack.Top();
        Assert.AreEqual(pushed, topped);
    }
}
```

That works, too.

Let's move on. The next test determines what happens when we call *Top* on a *Stack* that has no elements.

Test 11: Call *Top* on a *Stack* that has no elements.

Consistency is a key component of designing a class library. Because we chose to throw an *InvalidOperationException* when we called *Pop*, we should be consistent and throw the same exception when we call *Top*. Let's write the test:

```
[Test]
[ExpectedException(typeof(InvalidOperationException))]
public void TopEmptyStack()
{
    stack.Top();
}
```

Of course, this does not work. NUnit provides the details:

```
Tests run: 11, Failures: 1, Not run: 0, Time: 0.031263 seconds

Failures:
1) StackFixture.TopEmptyStack : Expected: InvalidOperationException but was
```

```
ArgumentOutOfRangeException
   at System.Collections.ArrayList.get_Item(Int32 index)
   at Stack.Top() in c:\projects\book\stack\stack.cs:line 33
   at StackFixture.TopEmptyStack() in c:\stackfixture.cs:line 119
```

You would think we would learn something—this is the same failure we got when we first implemented *Pop*. We need something similar in *Top*:

```
public object Top()
{
    if(IsEmpty) throw new
        InvalidOperationException("cannot top an empty stack");

    return elements[0];
}
```

This works. However, the similarity between *Top* and *Pop* is very apparent and needs to be refactored. They both check to see whether there are elements in the list and throw an exception if there aren't any. The best solution seems to have *Pop* call *Top*. Let's give that a try:

```
public object Pop()
{
    object top = Top();
    elements.RemoveAt(0);
    return top;
}

public object Top()
{
    if(IsEmpty)
        throw new InvalidOperationException("Stack is Empty");

    return elements[0];
}
```

This works: the duplication has been removed. We did have to make a change to the message that was in the exception—it is more generic now, which is a small price to pay for consistency in the code. We can now check this test off the list. (There are only three more to go, so the end is in sight.)

Test 12: *Push null* onto the *Stack* and verify that *IsEmpty* is false.

This is the first test that was added when we wrote the test that called *Pop* on an empty *Stack*. As you might recall, one of the options was to return a *null* to indicate that there were no elements in the *Stack*. If we had chosen that route, the programmer couldn't have stored *null* on the *Stack*, so the interface would be less explicit.

This test pushes *null* onto the *Stack* and verifies that *IsEmpty* is false:

```
[Test]
public void PushNull()
{
    stack.Push(null);
    Assert.IsFalse(stack.IsEmpty);
}
```

This works just fine. Let's do the next test.

Test 13: *Push null* onto the *Stack*, *Pop* the *Stack*, and verify that the value returned is *null*.

The previous test verified that *IsEmpty* was correct after pushing *null* onto the *Stack*. In this test, we push a *null* object onto the *Stack* and then call *Pop* to retrieve the element and remove it from the *Stack*. The value returned from *Pop* should be equal to *null*.

```
[Test]
public void PushNullCheckPop()
{
    stack.Push(null);
    Assert.IsNull(stack.Pop());
    Assert.IsTrue(stack.IsEmpty);
}
```

Let's compile and run the test. It works! This test has two asserts: one to check whether the return value is *null*, and one to check that *IsEmpty* is true. They could be done separately, but we chose to combine them because they are associated with the same test setup.

Now there is only one test left. Does the *Top* method work when we push *null* onto the *Stack?*

Test 14: Push *null* onto the *Stack*, call *Top*, and verify that the value returned is *null*.

In this test, we push a *null* object onto the *Stack* and then call *Top* to retrieve the element from the *Stack*. The value returned from *Top* should be equal to *null*.

```
[Test]
public void PushNullCheckTop()
{
```

```
    stack.Push(null);
    Assert.IsNull(stack.Top());
    Assert.IsFalse(stack.IsEmpty);
}
```

Compiling and running the tests indicate success. This is the last test on the list, and we can't think of any others. Although there are probably things we missed, we can't think of any for now—so the task is complete. We can check the code into the repository and work on the next task. As bugs are found, we will add other tests to cover the cases; this ensures that the test coverage will improve over time.

Summary

In this chapter, we built a *Stack* as an example of Test-Driven Development, and our version resulted in 14 tests. Reviewing the code shows that there is much more test code than actual code.

If you study the individual steps, you probably notice that we spent most of our time writing tests instead of writing the *Stack* code. This is because when we write tests, we focus on what the class does and how it is used instead of how it is implemented. This emphasis is very different from other ways of writing software, in which the code is written and then we figure out how to use it.

Comparing the size of the two classes is interesting. The *Stack* class is 35 lines of code; the *StackFixture* class contains 144 lines of code. The test code is more than four times the size of the *Stack* code. The following is the completed code in its entirety:

StackFixture.cs

```
using System;
using NUnit.Framework;

[TestFixture]
public class StackFixture
{
    private Stack stack;

    [SetUp]
    public void Init()
    {
```

```
        stack = new Stack();
    }

    [Test]
    public void Empty()
    {
        Assert.IsTrue(stack.IsEmpty);
    }

    [Test]
    public void PushOne()
    {
        stack.Push("first element");
        Assert.IsFalse(stack.IsEmpty,
            "After Push, IsEmpty should be false");
    }

    [Test]
    public void Pop()
    {
        stack.Push("first element");
        stack.Pop();
        Assert.IsTrue(stack.IsEmpty,
            "After Push - Pop, IsEmpty should be true");
    }

    [Test]
    public void PushPopContentCheck()
    {
        int expected = 1234;
        stack.Push(expected);
        int actual = (int)stack.Pop();
        Assert.AreEqual(expected, actual);
    }

    [Test]
    public void PushPopMultipleElements()
    {
        string pushed1 = "1";
        stack.Push(pushed1);
        string pushed2 = "2";
        stack.Push(pushed2);
        string pushed3 = "3";
        stack.Push(pushed3);

        string popped = (string)stack.Pop();
        Assert.AreEqual(pushed3, popped);
        popped = (string)stack.Pop();
```

```csharp
    Assert.AreEqual(pushed2, popped);
    popped = (string)stack.Pop();
    Assert.AreEqual(pushed1, popped);
}

[Test]
[ExpectedException(typeof(InvalidOperationException))]
public void PopEmptyStack()
{
    stack.Pop();
}

[Test]
public void PushTop()
{
    stack.Push("42");
    stack.Top();
    Assert.IsFalse(stack.IsEmpty);
}

[Test]
public void PushTopContentCheckOneElement()
{
    string pushed = "42";
    stack.Push(pushed);
    string topped = (string)stack.Top();
    Assert.AreEqual(pushed, topped);
}

[Test]
public void PushTopContentCheckMultiples()
{
    string pushed3 = "3";
    stack.Push(pushed3);
    string pushed4 = "4";
    stack.Push(pushed4);
    string pushed5 = "5";
    stack.Push(pushed5);

    string topped = (string)stack.Top();
    Assert.AreEqual(pushed5, topped);
}

[Test]
public void PushTopNoStackStateChange()
{
    string pushed = "44";
    stack.Push(pushed);
```

```
            for(int index = 0; index < 10; index++)
            {
                string topped = (string)stack.Top();
                Assert.AreEqual(pushed, topped);
            }
        }

        [Test]
        [ExpectedException(typeof(InvalidOperationException))]
        public void TopEmptyStack()
        {
            stack.Top();
        }

        [Test]
        public void PushNull()
        {
            stack.Push(null);
            Assert.IsFalse(stack.IsEmpty);
        }

        [Test]
        public void PushNullCheckPop()
        {
            stack.Push(null);
            Assert.IsNull(stack.Pop());
            Assert.IsTrue(stack.IsEmpty);
        }

        [Test]
        public void PushNullCheckTop()
        {
            stack.Push(null);
            Assert.IsNull(stack.Top());
            Assert.IsFalse(stack.IsEmpty);
        }
    }
```

Stack.cs

```
using System;
using System.Collections;

public class Stack
{
    private ArrayList elements = new ArrayList();

    public bool IsEmpty
```

```
    {
        get
        {
            return (elements.Count == 0);
        }
    }

    public void Push(object element)
    {
        elements.Insert(0, element);
    }

    public object Pop()
    {
        object top = Top();
        elements.RemoveAt(0);
        return top;
    }

    public object Top()
    {
        if(IsEmpty)
            throw new InvalidOperationException("Stack is Empty");

        return elements[0];
    }
}
```

3

Refactoring—By Example

In Chapters 1 and 2, we briefly touched on the subject of refactoring. This chapter gives a detailed treatment of this topic because refactoring is one of the fundamental aspects of test-driven development and a very useful practice in its own right.

Refactoring is an activity aimed at improving the internal structure of existing code without making externally visible changes to the functionality. Why would such changes be useful? (After all, there is an age-old engineering adage: "If it ain't broke, don't fix it.") Are we suggesting fixing a problem that does not exist? Is refactoring just another way to waste your time and money? The simple answer is no.

> **Note** Refactoring is a long-term, cost-efficient, and responsible approach to software ownership.

We argue that refactoring is the way to make your long-term software ownership less painful. Through refactoring, design intent becomes clearer as the code evolves. Without refactoring, the code's clarity will degrade over time, eventually becoming unintelligible.

Let's look at some code to clarify the point. We will demonstrate the basic ideas behind refactoring on a simple piece of code that is in need of some maintenance.

> **More Info**   For additional reading on this topic, read Martin Fowler's book: *Refactoring: Improving the Design of Existing Code* (Addison-Wesley, 1999). This book is the source of the refactoring names that are used in this chapter. As a side note, the examples in Martin's book are in Java but are straightforward enough to follow if you know C#.

The Sieve

The code we will refactor implements an algorithm to generate small prime numbers (say up to 10,000,000). The algorithm is called the *Sieve of Eratosthenes*. Make a list of all the integers less than or equal to n (and greater than one). Strike out the multiples of all primes less than or equal to the square root of n; the numbers that are left are the primes (*http://primes.utm.edu/glossary/page.php?sort=SieveOfEratosthenes*).

The existing implementation is shown here:

```
using System;
using System.Collections;

public class Primes
{
    public static ArrayList Generate(int maxValue)
    {
        ArrayList result = new ArrayList();

        int[] primes = GenerateArray(maxValue);
        for(int i = 0; i < primes.Length; ++i)
            result.Add(primes[i]);

        return result;
    }

    [Obsolete("This method is obsolete, use Generate instead")]
    public static int[] GenerateArray(int maxValue)
    {
        if(maxValue >= 2)
        {
            // declarations
            int s = maxValue + 1; // size of array
            bool[] f = new bool[s];
            int i;
```

```
    // initialize the array to true
    for(i=0; i<s; i++)
        f[i] = true;

    // get rid of known nonprimes
    f[0] = f[1] = false;

    // sieve
    int j;
    for(i=2; i<Math.Sqrt(s)+1; i++)
    {
        for(j=2*i; j<s; j+=i)
            f[j] = false; // multiple is not prime
    }

    // how many primes are there?
    int count = 0;
    for(i=0; i<s; i++)
        if(f[i]) // if prime
            count++; // bump count

    int[] primes = new int[count];

    // move the primes into the result
    for(i=0, j=0; i<s; i++)
    {
        if(f[i]) // if prime
            primes[j++] = i;
    }

    return primes;
    } // maxValue >= 2
    else
        return new int[0]; // return null array
    }
}
```

As you can see from the code, there are two methods defined to generate prime numbers. The first method, *Generate*, returns the prime numbers in an *ArrayList*. The second method, *GenerateArray*, was written to return an array of integers. The *GenerateArray* method is also marked with the *Obsolete* attribute, which is usually an indicator that the code will be removed when possible. It turns out that today is the day we will remove this function because the *GenerateArray* method is no longer called by the application code but it is still called by the *Generate* method. It looks like we won't be able to just delete it. Luckily, the code has a set of tests written using NUnit for it:

```csharp
using System;
using System.Collections;
using NUnit.Framework;

[TestFixture]
public class PrimesFixture
{
    private int[] knownPrimes = new int[]
    { 2, 3, 5, 7, 11, 13, 17, 19, 23, 29 };

    [Test]
    public void Zero()
    {
        int[] primes = Primes.GenerateArray(0);
        Assert.AreEqual(0, primes.Length);
    }

    [Test]
    public void ListZero()
    {
        ArrayList primes = Primes.Generate(0);
        Assert.AreEqual(0, primes.Count);
    }

    [Test]
    public void Single()
    {
        int[] primes = Primes.GenerateArray(2);
        Assert.AreEqual(1, primes.Length);
        Assert.AreEqual(2, primes[0]);
    }

    [Test]
    public void ListSingle()
    {
        ArrayList primes = Primes.Generate(2);
        Assert.AreEqual(1, primes.Count);
        Assert.IsTrue(primes.Contains(2));
    }

    [Test]
    public void Prime()
    {
        int[] centArray = Primes.GenerateArray(100);
        Assert.AreEqual(25, centArray.Length);
        Assert.AreEqual(97, centArray[24]);
    }
```

```
[Test]
public void ListPrime()
{
    ArrayList centList = Primes.Generate(100);
    Assert.AreEqual(25, centList.Count);
    Assert.AreEqual(97, centList[24]);
}

[Test]
public void Basic()
{
    int[] primes =
        Primes.GenerateArray(knownPrimes[knownPrimes.Length-1]);
    Assert.AreEqual(knownPrimes.Length, primes.Length);

    int i = 0;
    foreach(int prime in primes)
        Assert.AreEqual(knownPrimes[i++], prime);
}

[Test]
public void ListBasic()
{
    ArrayList primes =
        Primes.Generate(knownPrimes[knownPrimes.Length-1]);
    Assert.AreEqual(knownPrimes.Length, primes.Count);

    int i = 0;
    foreach(int prime in primes)
        Assert.AreEqual(knownPrimes[i++], prime);
}


[Test]
public void Lots()
{
    int bound = 10101;
    int[] primes = Primes.GenerateArray(bound);

    foreach(int prime in primes)
        Assert.IsTrue(IsPrime(prime), "is prime");

    foreach(int prime in primes)
    {
        if(IsPrime(prime))
            Assert.IsTrue(Contains(prime, primes),
                "contains primes");
        else
```

```
                    Assert.IsFalse(Contains(prime, primes),
                        "doesn't contain composites");
        }
    }

    [Test]
    public void ListLots()
    {
        int bound = 10101;
        ArrayList primes = Primes.Generate(bound);
        foreach(int prime in primes)
            Assert.IsTrue(IsPrime(prime), "is prime");

        foreach(int prime in primes)
        {
            if(IsPrime(prime))
                Assert.IsTrue(primes.Contains(prime),
                    "contains primes");
            else
                Assert.IsFalse(primes.Contains(prime),
                    "doesn't contain composites");
        }
    }


    private static bool IsPrime(int n)
    {
        if(n < 2) return false;

        bool result = true;
        double x = Math.Sqrt(n);
        int i = 2;
        while(result && i <= x)
        {
            result = (0 != n % i);
            i += 1;
        }

        return result;
    }


    private static bool Contains(int value, int[] primes)
    {
            return (Array.IndexOf(primes, value) != -1);
    }
}
```

Before Refactoring the Code: Make Sure It All Works

It is important to remember that refactoring has to be done in conjunction with running tests for the code being refactored. After all, refactoring is not supposed to change the externally observable functionality of the code being refactored. The tests are the tools needed to verify such functionality. So the first step of the refactoring process is to run the tests before you make any code changes.

Let's run the tests. All of them pass, so we can begin from a known good state.

Refactoring Cycle

The cycle we will follow is straightforward: Identify a problem, select a refactoring to address the problem, apply the refactoring by making the appropriate code change; compile and run the tests; repeat. The emphasis is on the code changes being very small—and running the tests. Why small changes? We transition the system from a known good state to the next desirable state.

Think of it as climbing a wall. If the wall is high, you might break your neck attempting to climb it, but you could use a ladder to assist you. With a ladder in place if you feel tired, you can just stop and rest. The tests are your ladder—they are both your safety net and a climbing tool. So, before you start climbing, what should you do? Do yourself a favor: Make sure that your ladder is not broken. This brings us to the following rule for refactoring:

> **Important**   As you refactor your code, make sure that the tests are up-to-date. If you need to change them to reflect the changing requirements, do it first.

In short, maintain your ladder. Let's take a look at the tests.

Refactoring 0: Remove Unneeded Code

There are five test methods for the *array*-based version and five test methods for the *ArrayList* version. Because the *GenerateArray* method is being removed, it appears that we can remove the tests for that method. We can do this safely because we are not losing any test coverage by removing the *array*-based tests. The *ArrayList*-based tests are exact duplicates in terms of what is being tested.

After the *array*-based tests are removed, the following tests remain:

- *ListZero*

- *ListSingle*

- *ListPrime*

- *ListBasic*

- *ListLots*

We can also get rid of the utility method *Contains* because it was used only by the *array*-based tests. After we finish removing the code, we compile and run the tests. The test method count drops to five and we have a green bar, so it is time to move on.

Refactoring 1: Rename Method

The next refactoring is still in the test code. After we remove the *array*-based tests, there is no need to preface each method with the word *List*. We need to implement the "Rename method" of refactoring. The reasoning is that you should call an apple an apple; no need to call it a "green apple" unless the greenness of the apple is of the essence. Meaningful method names are important for code readability and in turn its overall maintainability. In short, method names should convey their intentions.

Here is the test code after each method has been renamed; the contents of the methods have not changed, so they are not shown here:

```
using System;
using System.Collections;
using NUnit.Framework;

[TestFixture]
public class PrimesFixture
{
    private int[] knownPrimes = new int[]
    { 2, 3, 5, 7, 11, 13, 17, 19, 23, 29 };

    [Test]
    public void Zero()
    {
      // …
    }

    [Test]
    public void Single()
    {
      // …
    }
```

```
[Test]
public void Prime()
{
  // …
}

[Test]
public void Basic()
{
  // …
}


[Test]
public void Lots()
{
  // …
}


private static bool IsPrime(int n)
{
  // …
}
}
```

In this case, the renaming of the methods is straightforward. There should be no code calling the test methods. The more general case is a bit more complicated because you might have to change the callers of the method being renamed. Modern development environments make it easier to accomplish this task and pretty much take care of the process of finding and replacing the method names. If you are using a simple text editor, you might let your compiler tell you which classes you need to fix (which is crude, but it works). As always, after we make the changes, we compile and run the tests. The tests passed, so it's time to continue.

Refactoring 2: Add a Test

The *Single* test method verifies that 2 is a prime number; the *Zero* test method verifies that 0 is not a prime number. What about the number 1? We should also have a test that ensures that 1 is not a prime number.

We add a new test named *ZeroOne* and rename the *Single* method to be *ZeroTwo* to reflect the range of values being tested:

```
[Test]
public void ZeroOne()
{
    ArrayList primes = Primes.Generate(1);
    Assert.AreEqual(0, primes.Count);
}

[Test]
public void ZeroTwo()
{
    ArrayList primes = Primes.Generate(2);
    Assert.AreEqual(1, primes.Count);
    Assert.IsTrue(primes.Contains(2));
}
```

Now we have three methods that test the special cases of 0, 1, and 2. They look very similar, but it is not apparent how to factor out any commonality. When we compile and run all the tests, they succeed. We now have six tests.

When Are We Finished?

At every step of the way, an important question to ask is "Am I finished?" By the very nature of moving from a known good state to the next state, it is possible to stop at any time. What is there left to do? Why didn't we stop after removing the *array*-based tests? Because we immediately saw what we could not possibly see before: the method names could be improved. Each simple refactoring we implement opens up opportunities for further refactorings to make the code communicate its intentions more clearly.

What makes the process interesting is that it is a process of discovery. We probably don't know what refactoring we'll implement next. We also don't create a grand plan of 1001 refactorings that are needed to make this code better. We let the code itself drive the process. The code tells us which refactoring is needed at the appropriate time, and it evolves gradually into the shape it wants to take over time. The answer for now is that we are not done. We have not removed the *array*-based implementation. However, we are done with refactoring the test code.

Refactoring 3: Hide Method

Let's look at the code that generates the prime numbers. The *GenerateArray* method is used internally by the *Generate* method. There is no need to keep it public any more. We'll implement the "Hide method" refactoring, which is quite simple. In C#, it is accomplished by changing the visibility of the method from *public* to *private*. The following code

```
public static int[] GenerateArray(int maxValue)
```

now becomes

```
private static int[] GenerateArray(int maxValue)
```

Why did we do this refactoring? The less the code promises, the easier it is to deliver. The *GenerateArray* method now becomes an implementation detail. The code compiles and the tests pass, so let's move on to the next step.

Refactoring 4: Replace Nested Conditional with Guard Clauses

Large monitors with high resolutions allow you to see many more lines of code onscreen than you could a few years ago. But you won't make many friends if you continue to write (or tolerate) code like the *GenerateArray* method.

What is the biggest problem with the *GenerateArray* method? Let's distill it down to the essence:

```
if(maxValue >= 2)
{
       pages and pages of code that won't fit on your screen
       return primes;
} // maxValue >= 2
else
       return new int[0]; // return null array
```

The problem is that when you finally get to the *else* statement, the *if* statement has probably scrolled off the screen, so you do not have the context in which the statement is being executed. One way to correct this problem is to use the "Replace nested conditional with a guard clause" refactoring. Employing a guard clause at the beginning of the method dispenses with the bad input and focuses the method on processing the good input. Changing the method to use a guard clause looks like this:

```
if(maxValue < 2) return new int[0];

the rest of the code here.
```

Those of you who subscribe to one of the major tenets of structured programming (single entry point/single exit point) are probably jumping out of your chair. The reason this other approach is all right in this situation is because the guard clause identifies a rare situation that can be handled immediately. This frees up the rest of the code to handle the typical calling scenario without having to worry about the rare or invalid situations. In short, with the guard clause in place, the code is easier to read. After we insert the guard clause, the code compiles and the tests pass.

Refactoring 5: Inline Method

Now that the only code that calls *GenerateArray* is the *Generate* method, we can use the "Inline method" refactoring to put the method's body into the body of its caller and completely remove the method. This is not a license to create huge methods. If we intended to stop refactoring after inlining this method, we would argue to not inline the method.

The point that needs to be stressed is communication. If it makes sense to inline a method because it communicates the intent better than it did previously, you should do it. It also decreases the surface area of the code, which should improve its testability if you don't have huge methods. Because the *Generate* method returns an *ArrayList* and the *GenerateArray* method returns an *array*, we will need to slightly alter the guard clause introduced in the previous step to return an empty *ArrayList* instead of an empty *array*. Here is the *Generate* method after inlining the *GenerateArray* method (the modified guard clause is in boldface):

```
public static ArrayList Generate(int maxValue)
{
    ArrayList result = new ArrayList();
    if(maxValue < 2) return result;

    // declarations
    int s = maxValue + 1; // size of array
    bool[] f = new bool[s];
    int i;

    // initialize the array to true
    for(i=0; i<s; i++)
        f[i] = true;

    // get rid of known nonprimes
    f[0] = f[1] = false;

    // sieve
    int j;
    for(i=2; i<Math.Sqrt(s)+1; i++)
    {
        for(j=2*i; j<s; j+=i)
            f[j] = false; // multiple is not prime
    }

    // how many primes are there?
    int count = 0;
    for(i=0; i<s; i++)
        if(f[i]) // if prime
```

```
        count++; // bump count

    int[] primes = new int[count];

    // move the primes into the result
    for(i=0, j=0; i<s; i++)
    {
        if(f[i]) // if prime
            primes[j++] = i;
    }

    for(i = 0; i < primes.Length; ++i)
        result.Add(primes[i]);

    return result;
}
```

This refactoring often requires more effort due to local variable name clashes. When performing this refactoring, you will find it useful to comment out the method that is being inlined instead of deleting it. After the code compiles and the tests pass, you can safely delete the commented-out code, which is useful to go back to in case your tests do not pass. You could also use your source-code control system to achieve the same benefit.

The code compiles, and the tests pass. The *GenerateArray* function has now been removed (or to be more exact, consumed, by the *Generate* method). Remember, this was the objective of the task. We could stop right now and be finished. However, we are still left with the legacy of the *array*-based implementation, which is filled with bad variable names and loops that iterate over the list of numbers many times. We need to do some more work to get this code in better shape.

Refactoring 6: Rename Variable

Looking at the code in the *Generate* method, we see several variables whose names do not communicate much about their intended uses, so we should give them more descriptive names. For example, what does the variable f mean? Does f indicate that the number is prime or not prime? Let's take a look at the following code snippet to demonstrate the point:

```
if(f[i]) // if prime
```

Instead of having comments in the code describing what the variable f means, it is better to give the variable a more descriptive name. In almost all cases in the existing program, every time the variable f is used there is an associated comment. Let's remove the need for the comment by providing a more descriptive variable name. The name *isPrime* describes what the variable means in the code more clearly. After the name is changed, we can remove the comment because the variable name is descriptive enough:

```
public static ArrayList Generate(int maxValue)
{
    ArrayList result = new ArrayList();

    if(maxValue < 2) return result;

    // declarations
    int s = maxValue + 1; // size of array
    bool[] isPrime = new bool[s];
    int i;

    for(i=0; i<s; i++)
        isPrime[i] = true;

    isPrime[0] = isPrime[1] = false;

    // sieve
    int j;
    for(i=2; i<Math.Sqrt(s)+1; i++)
    {
        for(j=2*i; j<s; j+=i)
            isPrime[j] = false; // multiple is not prime
    }

    // how many primes are there?
    int count = 0;
    for(i=0; i<s; i++)
        if(isPrime[i])
            count++; // bump count

    int[] primes = new int[count];

    // move the primes into the result
    for(i=0, j=0; i<s; i++)
    {
        if(isPrime[i])
            primes[j++] = i;
    }

    for(i = 0; i < primes.Length; ++i)
        result.Add(primes[i]);

    return result;
}
```

The changes are made, the code compiles, and the tests pass. It does not look as if we are finished, however. The code still has a lot of the remnants of the *array*-based implementation and it still has many loops that seem as if they all iterate over the same elements.

Refactoring 7: Collapse Loops

Looking at the last few lines of the *Generate* method, you can see two loops doing almost entirely the same thing. Here is the existing code:

```
int[] primes = new int[count];

// move the primes into the result
for(i=0, j=0; i<s; i++)
{
    if(isPrime[i])
        primes[j++] = i;
}

for(i = 0; i < primes.Length; ++i)
    result.Add(primes[i]);
```

The first loop cycles through the *isPrime* array to create a new array named *primes*. The second loop cycles through the *primes* array to build the list. This is a remnant of the *array*-based implementation returning an *array* and the *ArrayList* function converting it into an *ArrayList*. Because we no longer return an array, we can do this without creating the *primes* array, as follows:

```
for(i = 0; i < s; ++i)
{
    if(isPrime[i])
        result.Add(i);
}
```

After this change is made, the code compiles and the test passes.

Refactoring 8: Remove Dead Code

The *array*-based legacy is almost gone. Because we no longer create the *primes* array, we no longer need the *count* variable because it was just used to size the *primes* array. Therefore, we can get rid of the *count* variable and the loop that calculates it. Let's move on.

Refactoring 9: Collapse Loops (Again)

Are we done? We could be, but it appears as if a few more changes could make the code a lot clearer, so let's continue for awhile longer.

Look at this loop:

```
for(i=2; i<Math.Sqrt(s)+1; i++)
{
    for(j=2*i; j<s; j+=i)
        isPrime[j] = false; // multiple is not prime
}
```

Can we make it better? The algorithm states that you have to remove multiples only if the number is a prime number, so the code is not as efficient as it could be. Try this:

```
for(i=2; i<Math.Sqrt(s)+1; i++)
{
    if(isPrime[i])
    {
        for(j=2*i; j<s; j+=i)
            isPrime[j] = false; // multiple is not prime
    }
}
```

We make the change, compile, and run the tests. They pass, so adding this did not have an impact on the functionality, and the code is closer to the intent of the algorithm.

We Can Do Some More...

Is the code faster? Probably, but because we do not have a performance test, we do not know the answer to that. However, after we make this change, the two loops at the bottom of the program look very similar; they have the same *if* statement in them. Perhaps we can collapse the two loops together.

Here's the existing code:

```
int j;
for(i = 2; i < Math.Sqrt(s)+1; i++)
{
    if(isPrime[i])
    {
        for(j=2*i; j<s; j+=i)
            isPrime[j] = false; // multiple is not prime
    }
}

for(i = 0; i < s; ++i)
{
```

```
        if(isPrime[i])
            result.Add(i);
    }
```

The boundaries of the loops are different. The first loop iterates over the *isPrime* array, beginning at 2 and continuing to *Math.Sqrt(s) + 1*. The second loop iterates over the *isPrime* array, starting at 0 and continuing all the way to *s*.

Enough about symbols. Let's look at real numbers. If *s* were equal to 100, the first loop would execute 10 times, and the second loop would execute 100 times. It looks as if it would be simple to have the second loop start at 2 instead of 0. Let's make that change. All the tests pass, so it works and the lower boundary conditions are now the same.

Now what about the upper boundary? It looks as if we could change the first loop to continue all the way to *s*. This is clearly less efficient, but (as stated previously) it is hard to say whether that is a problem because the code does not have a performance test. Let's change the code to the following and see whether it works:

```
int j;
for(i = 2; i < s; i++)
{
    if(isPrime[i])
    {
        for(j=2*i; j<s; j+=i)
            isPrime[j] = false; // multiple is not prime
    }
}

for(i = 2; i < s; i++)
{
    if(isPrime[i])
        result.Add(i);
}
```

All the tests pass, and the loops have identical boundary conditions. It is clearer now, after looking at the code and knowing that the tests run successfully, that we can safely collapse the loops into a single loop.

```
int j;
for(i = 2; i < s; i++)
{
    if(isPrime[i])
    {
        result.Add(i);
        for(j=2*i; j<s; j+=i)
            isPrime[j] = false; // multiple is not prime
    }
}
```

That works—the tests passed. It is difficult to say that the code is less efficient because we did get rid of the second loop. And we removed a couple of other loops that were used in the *array*-based implementation, so it is possible that what we have now is more efficient than it used to be. We leave it up to you to verify whether the code performs worse now than it did before we started.

Refactoring 10: Reduce Local Variable Scope

Because of all the previous refactorings, the variable *j* is now used in only one loop. We can now change its scope by moving its declaration into the loop where it is used:

```
for(i = 2; i < s; i++)
{
    if(isPrime[i])
    {
        result.Add(i);
        for(int j = 2 * i; j < s; j += i)
            isPrime[j] = false; // multiple is not prime
    }
}
```

That works just fine, and the local variable *j*'s scope is diminished.

Refactoring 11: Replace Temp with Query

The next step is to replace the temporary variable *s* because it does not communicate what it actually means:

```
int s = maxValue + 1; // size of array
```

Instead of a temporary variable, we can replace the variable entirely by using the expression *isPrime.Length,* which communicates what we really mean and is already provided by the array implementation. The changes are in boldface as follows:

```
public static ArrayList Generate(int maxValue)
{
    ArrayList result = new ArrayList();

    if(maxValue < 2) return result;

    bool[] isPrime = new bool[maxValue+1];
    int i;

    for(i = 0; i < isPrime.Length; i++)
```

```
            isPrime[i] = true;

        isPrime[0] = isPrime[1] = false;

        // sieve
        for(i = 2; i < isPrime.Length; i++)
        {
            if(isPrime[i])
            {
                result.Add(i);
                for(int j = 2 * i; j < isPrime.Length; j += i)
                    isPrime[j] = false; // multiple is not prime
            }
        }

        return result;
    }
```

Refactoring 12: Remove Dead Code

There still is some code that is not used any more due to the collapse of loops done a few refactorings ago. Because the loop that does the sieve process starts at 2 and we load the list from within that loop, we no longer need to initialize 0 and 1 to *false* because they are never accessed. We can safely remove the following line:

```
    isPrime[0] = isPrime[1] = false;
```

The tests pass when we compile and run them, so it was probably safe to assume that we could remove the line.

Refactoring 13: Extract Method

Even though the code has come a long way, there is still room for improvement, especially for making the code much more explicit about what it is doing. For example, look at the boldface code in the following snippet:

```
for(i = 2; i < isPrime.Length; i++)
{
    if(isPrime[i])
    {
        result.Add(i);
        for(int j = 2 * i; j < isPrime.Length; j += i)
            isPrime[j] = false; // multiple is not prime
    }
}
```

What does the highlighted loop do? It is clear what the loop does; there is a code comment explaining what it does. The comment is a good indicator that the code does not communicate its intent directly. It needs the comment to say what it does.

> **Note**   When you see a block of code with a comment attached to it, it is often a good idea to extract that code into a method and make sure that the method's name conveys the meaning specified by the comment.

Let's extract the boldface code into its own method named *RemoveMultiples*:

```
private static void RemoveMultiples(int prime, bool[] isPrime)
{
    for(int j = 2 * prime; j < isPrime.Length; j += prime)
        isPrime[j] = false;
}
```

After the method is extracted, we need to modify the code to use it. Here is the modified code:

```
for(i = 2; i < isPrime.Length; i++)
{
    if(isPrime[i])
    {
        result.Add(i);
        RemoveMultiples(i, isPrime);
    }
}
```

Instead of needing the comment, the method name communicates exactly what it is doing.

Refactoring 14: Extract Method (Again)

The code is getting smaller and smaller with more explicitly named methods and variables; in fact, we can now see that there are two stages in the algorithm: initialization and elimination. Let's extract the elimination portion into a method called *Sieve* using the "Extract method" refactoring (the changes are boldface):

```
public static ArrayList Generate(int maxValue)
{
    ArrayList result = new ArrayList();
```

```
    if(maxValue < 2) return result;

    bool[] isPrime = new bool[maxValue+1];
    int i;

    for(i = 0; i < isPrime.Length; i++)
        isPrime[i] = true;

    Sieve(isPrime, result);

    return result;
}

private static void Sieve(bool[] isPrime, ArrayList result)
{
    for(int i = 2; i < isPrime.Length; i++)
    {
        if(isPrime[i])
        {
            result.Add(i);
            RemoveMultiples(i, isPrime);
        }
    }
}

private static void RemoveMultiples(int prime, bool[] isPrime)
{
    for(int j = 2 * prime; j < isPrime.Length; j += prime)
        isPrime[j] = false;
}
```

The code is much more explicit. Before we go on, however, let's make one more change. The *Sieve* function can return the *ArrayList* instead of getting it passed to it; as you see here:

```
public static ArrayList Generate(int maxValue)
{
    if(maxValue < 2) return new ArrayList();

    bool[] isPrime = new bool[maxValue+1];
    int i;

    for(i = 0; i < isPrime.Length; i++)
        isPrime[i] = true;

    return Sieve(isPrime);
}
```

```
private static ArrayList Sieve(bool[] isPrime)
{
    ArrayList result = new ArrayList();

    for(int i = 2; i < isPrime.Length; i++)
    {
        if(isPrime[i])
        {
            result.Add(i);
            RemoveMultiples(i, isPrime);
        }
    }

    return result;
}

private static void RemoveMultiples(int prime, bool[] isPrime)
{
    for(int j = 2 * prime; j < isPrime.Length; j += prime)
        isPrime[j] = false;
}
```

Refactoring 15: Reduce Local Variable Scope

Because we extracted a method that used the variable i, we can reduce the scope of the variable in the *Generate* method. The following code

```
int i;
for(i=0; i < isPrime.Length; i++)
    isPrime[i] = true;
```

now becomes

```
for(int i=0; i < isPrime.Length; i++)
        isPrime[i] = true;
```

Even though the step is small, it is still important to compile the code and run the tests. If you don't, you could have a failure a couple of steps ahead and not know exactly what was changed.

Refactoring 16: Convert Procedural Design to Objects

We previously discussed the two steps in the algorithm: initialization and elimination. There is also a variable, *isPrime*, that is shared between the two stages. So we have the following:

- State (*isPrime*)

- Logic to initialize the state

- Logic to operate on the state

This set of conditions sounds as if we need an object to hold this state, a constructor to initialize the state, and a method to manipulate this state. Meet the next refactoring: "Convert procedural design to objects." This step is a little bit larger, so it probably makes sense to comment out the existing code first so that we have something to fall back on if we fail. Another alternative is to check the file into your source code control system and then make the change. If you fail, you can easily roll back to the previous version. The code after the refactoring looks like this:

```
public static ArrayList Generate(int maxValue)
{
    if(maxValue < 2) return new ArrayList();

    Primes primes = new Primes(maxValue);
    return primes.Sieve();
}

private bool[] isPrime;

private Primes(int maxValue)
{
    isPrime = new bool[maxValue+1];

    for(int i = 0; i < isPrime.Length; i++)
        isPrime[i] = true;
}

private ArrayList Sieve()
{
    ArrayList result = new ArrayList();

    for(int i = 2; i < isPrime.Length; i++)
    {
        if(isPrime[i])
        {
            result.Add(i);
            RemoveMultiples(i, isPrime);
        }
    }

    return result;
}
```

```
private void RemoveMultiples(int prime, bool[] isPrime)
{
    for(int j = 2 * prime; j < isPrime.Length; j += prime)
        isPrime[j] = false;
}
```

We really did not write a lot of new code; we just moved what we had around a bit. After we compiled and ran the tests, they did pass the first time. We then went back and removed the commented-out code. We are definitely getting close to a point of diminishing returns, but let's move on.

Refactoring 17: Keep the Data Close to Where It Is Used

For the first time, the code actually looks like object-oriented code. What a departure from what we had! Now that we have an object, we can see that the *Sieve* method could do a bit more, and the *Generate* method might do a bit less. The guard clause from the *Generate* method can be tucked away into the *Sieve* method to fully encapsulate the algorithm. Here is the code after applying this refactoring:

```
public static ArrayList Generate(int maxValue)
{
    Primes primes = new Primes(maxValue);
    return primes.Sieve();
}

private bool[] isPrime;

private Primes(int maxValue)
{
    isPrime = new bool[maxValue+1];

    for(int i = 0; i < isPrime.Length; i++)
        isPrime[i] = true;
}

private ArrayList Sieve()
{
    if(isPrime.Length < 2) return new ArrayList();

    ArrayList result = new ArrayList();
    for(int i = 2; i < isPrime.Length; i++)
    {
        if(isPrime[i])
        {
            result.Add(i);
```

```
        RemoveMultiples(i, isPrime);
      }
    }

    return result;
}

private void RemoveMultiples(int prime, bool[] isPrime)
{
    for(int j = 2 * prime; j < isPrime.Length; j += prime)
        isPrime[j] = false;
}
```

After scanning the code, there really isn't much left to do, so we are finished.

Summary

In this chapter, we demonstrated the following points:

- Refactoring allows the design of the code to improve by following a series of simple steps. For example, in this chapter we went from bad procedural code to a cleaner object-oriented implementation— while staying close to the green bar and without a large-scale rewrite. When you write your code, we expect you will refactor as you discover the need for it (not when it's too late and the code is so messed-up that it is more appealing just to throw it away and write it anew). The more "paranoid" you are about all the little problems in the code, the more proactive you will be in correcting them when you notice them rather than waiting until you have a big job on your hands.

- There was no mention of a debugger. Due to the small steps and the ability to verify them with the tests, you will not have to spend as much time debugging the software because changes can easily be rolled back to the previous state.

- The ability to do refactoring is a benefit that you receive from your investment in tests. The tests provide the safety net that enables the routine maintenance of the program. These tests allow you to alter the code without worrying about whether or not you have broken it.

Without the tests, you would not be able to move as quickly or as incrementally through this problem. In fact, you probably would have scrapped the whole thing and rewritten it.

■ You should not turn your "pragmatic paranoia" into a "morbid obsession." Your goal, after all, is to write software efficiently and not get stuck tweaking existing code into unattainable "perfection." When do you stop refactoring? There is no simple and fast rule here that we can offer. The general rule of thumb is that you need to refactor whatever code duplication you discover and move toward code that clearly communicates your intentions. And if you have some amount of code duplication that serves the goal of clearly communicating your intentions, it is all right to keep it.

■ Last, the order in which we did the refactorings is only an example. There are many other ways this code could be refactored and many other possible implementations. The main point driven home by the series of steps is that the code is the primary feedback mechanism for possible future refactorings.

Part II

Test-Driven Development Example

4

The Media Library Example

In this chapter, we introduce the media library example application, which is the example that we will use throughout the rest of the book to illustrate how to do Test-Driven Development (TDD) when developing a real world application. The example application approximates an actual application, but it does not have the complete functionality of a finished application.

With this example, we want to depart from a common practice of omitting some of the "difficult" aspects of real application development—such as error handling, robustness, performance, interoperability, evolving design around the legacy system requirements, and so on. However, to make such an example possible within the constraints of a book, we had to make compromises. We chose to reduce the features of the application but present a complete architectural crosscut. Much more functionality would be required before the software would really be released. Because our intent is that this application can evolve into the actual application, the design and implementation of what we present is intended to be production-ready. The code you see should handle errors correctly and be a suitable design with which you can build to complete the application.

The Skinny

Our fictitious company has a large existing database of musical recordings. The content of the database is sold to other companies to build user-friendly applications. To keep the data as current as possible, we sell updates to the data on a quarterly basis. Because new recordings are released weekly, the quarterly updates are out-of-date almost immediately and insufficient according to our customers. The far-too-infrequent updates cause customers to insert new recordings in their own copies of the data. These updates are done manually, and the data entered are not always "clean." (They include mistyped recording titles and incomplete track information, to name a few problems.) When our quarterly updates arrive, the database administrator has to merge the changes from our update into their database. Such merging is usually painful because of the dirty data and it often requires manual intervention by the database administrator.

Also, the customers forward the changes they have made to the content to us for inclusion in the next quarterly update. Our company is responsible for verifying the quality of this data and including the validated update into the next quarterly update that is distributed to all our customers. Some of our customers submit their changes late, and because of the required verification and merging, some updates might miss the deadlines to the quarterly update schedules (making our customers unhappy).

To improve the timeliness of the data, we decided to provide direct access to the clean data in our database while we preserve our control over the integrity of the data. To do this, we decided to build a service-based architecture around our data to provide the customers with a constantly updated repository of musical recordings. Our goal is to eliminate the need for the customers to maintain their own copies of the database. Another goal is to allow our customers to do updates to the data in the master database as they do now in their local copies, but to reduce the overhead on our side associated with the merging of such updates with updates of other customers.

One thing to keep in mind is that our customers deploy their solutions on a number of different platforms, so it is imperative that whatever we provide must be interoperable with our system. To that end, we intend to use Web services as the means of interoperability for access to the data. We will also provide a browser-based client to allow customers to insert new recordings and edit existing ones.

Existing Database

By far, the largest constraint is the existing database. Our company has been selling this database, which is hosted in Microsoft SQL Server 2000, for the past few years. It contains hundreds of thousands of recordings with millions of tracks. For this project, the database administrators of our database do not see why they should change the schema. We currently do not have any requirements that would cause us to change the schema, but the database administrators do not want us to change it. Therefore, we will view the schema as a constraint that we have to live with for the project. If it becomes a critical issue, we might raise it again later, but with some data to back up our needs. The existing data model is shown in Figure 4-1.

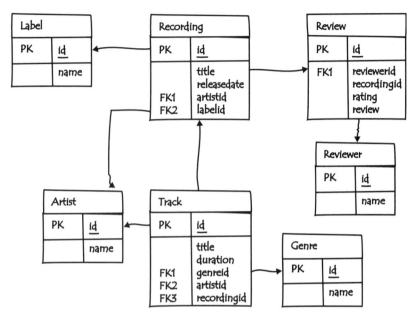

Figure 4-1   Recordings data model

The following sections briefly explain this data model.

Entities

The two primary entities in our data model are Recording and Track. A Recording is something that is publicly released by a music company on some type of media (compact disc, audiocassette, vinyl, and so on); this company is referred to in the model as a Label. A Track is a complete song. Each Recording also has a title and the date on which it was released. Each Track has a title and duration.

We also have a few secondary entities in our model that we use mostly to normalize the relational data:

Genre   This entity represents different musical styles; for example, rock, classical, pop, hip hop, and so on.

Artist   This entity is the name of the person or group that is the performer.

Label   This entity is the company that released the recording.

Review   This entity, which describes a critique of the recording, is written by a Reviewer. (Each reviewer has a name.)

Entity Relationships

Each Recording has many Tracks, one Label, one Artist, and many Reviews. Each Track has an Artist and a Genre. Each Review has one Reviewer. We have a special category of "Various Artists" to use as the artist for Recordings and Tracks performed by more than one artist. In the current model, we do not support individual track Reviews.

In Figure 4-1, the rightmost column in each table has special constraints associated with the corresponding attribute (listed in the leftmost column). For example, in the Track table, you see the *PK* (short for primary key) constraint associated with the *trackId* attribute, which means that the *trackId* attribute serves as the primary key in our database Track table. Similarly, the *FKx* (which stands for foreign key) constraint is used to describe a relationship between two entities. For example, the Track table has a foreign key constraint—*FK1*—associated with the *genreId* attribute to indicate that this attribute is used to capture an association between a Track and its Genre.

The First Feature

The first and highest priority feature that we need to implement involves accessing our database from anywhere on the Internet. As stated previously, we do not specify directly which platforms our customers use, so whatever access mechanism we come up with must be interoperable with their systems. To this end, we plan to use an ASP.NET Web service to retrieve recording information from our database.

The different aspects of the Web service implementation are detailed in Chapters 5, 6, and 7. Chapter 5, "Programmer Tests: Using TDD with ADO.NET" focuses on the implementation of a Data Access Layer using ADO.NET within the context of the solution. Chapter 6, "Programmer Tests: Using TDD with ASP.NET Web Services," describes the Web service portions of the feature. Finally, Chapter 7, "Customer Tests: Completing the First Feature," focuses on tests written by the customer using an open source testing tool called FIT (*http://fit.c2.com*). These tests are used to verify that the story is implemented correctly from the customer's perspective.

We really did not implement the feature in the order that is documented in the chapters. We started out on the client, and we eventually accessed the database and returned values one test at a time. However, the number of steps and the amount of detail that needs to be shown is overwhelming (and frankly pretty boring). We know because we tried it that way first, and we fell asleep writing it. Therefore, we choose to make the chapters more topical instead of using the narrative approach. Describing the solution in this manner also allows us to show aspects of testing that might not be needed for the solution but are important things to keep in mind when writing tests.

Additional Features

Chapter 8, "Driving Development with Customer Tests," introduces the ability to associate a review with an existing recording. For this feature, we need to provide some additional Web services, and we need to be able to modify the existing database. We also see how easy it is to extend the existing functionality to be able to support the new feature.

Chapter 9, "Driving Development with Customer Tests: Exposing a Failure Condition," describes an unsolved issue that was not fully addressed in Chapter 8. The issue arises when a user tries to add a review to a recording that the reviewer has already reviewed. This should not be allowed by the system. In this chapter, we first specify the problem by writing new customer and programmer tests. After the tests fail, we implement a solution. This solution is relevant to the database access layer as well as the services.

Chapter 10, "Programmer Tests: Using Transactions," continues the theme of the previous chapters by solving a problem that was caused by improper updates to the database, including issues with the programmer tests as well as the customer tests. The main issue is related to the program adding a Reviewer entity when a Review is created. If for some reason the Review is not added properly, we should automatically delete the Reviewer entity, so there should never be a Reviewer entity without a Review. The code that we implemented in Chapters 8 and 9 did just this. The solution that is implemented in this chapter uses the transaction support in SQL Server to remedy this problem. It also demonstrates the extensibility of the solution by allowing the relatively easy insertion of transaction support after the code has been written.

Chapter 11, "Service Layer Refactoring," addresses the need to move common functions that were developed in Chapters 8 through 10 into a new layer, called a Service Layer. We build this new layer as part of the last feature, which is to implement a Web client (which we focus on in Chapter 12, "Implementing a Web Client"). This chapter demonstrates the evolving nature of the architecture based on new functionality. We also address dependency management, which is important when building layered software architectures.

Chapter 12 describes how to write programmer tests when implementing an ASP.NET Web client. The chapter addresses the issues associated with writing tests for user interfaces.

5

Programmer Tests: Using TDD with ADO.NET

In this chapter, we demonstrate how to write programmer tests when implementing a data access layer using ADO.NET. We limit the scope of this chapter by implementing only functionality that is needed to implement the data access aspects of the Web service. (See Chapter 4, "The Media Library Example" for a more complete discussion of the feature.) As you will see, not only do we have to implement the functionality associated with the feature, we have to augment the solution to be able to write tests appropriately. In later chapters, this implementation will evolve to address additional capabilities such as transactions, concurrency, and updates.

Testing the Database Access Layer

Testing a program that accesses data stored in a database has a number of challenges that are different from those we described previously.

■   **Test time**   It takes significantly longer to run tests associated with data stored in a database than it does to run tests on in-memory data. The difference can easily be several orders of magnitude. Due to the increased amount of time it takes to execute the tests, you will see us use larger steps (more code) in this chapter to cut down on the number of times that we have to interact with the database.

■ **Consistency**   The database ensures that data stored within it is consistent with the schema definition. This consistency checking is an issue when writing tests. Ideally, we want to be able to test each entity without having to create all the supporting objects. However, due to the consistency checks, we have to create all the supporting objects just to test the individual entity. In this chapter, we will show you how using a typed *DataSet* can mitigate this problem.

■ **Test responsibility**   The test has to make sure that the environment in which it executes is known before the test is run. This means that it should not rely on any data already in the database. If you rely on data already in the database, you could run into trouble if another developer is manipulating the data at the same time or if it has changed since the last time you ran your tests. Therefore, prior to each test, you should insert into the database whatever is needed for your test, run your test, and then remove anything that was inserted. The amount of work needed in each test results in larger steps (more code). In this chapter, we use this technique for testing the individual entities and their relationships. This problem could be solved by each developer having his own copy of the database and a way to reset it to a known state during the setup of the test. A more advanced technique using transactions is also possible and will be presented in Chapter 10, "Programmer Tests: Using Transactions."

■ **Production database**   You should not run your programmer tests on the production database. The risk is too high that you will mess up the existing data. That said, how can you approximate the run-time environment for your tests? Running the tests on blank databases is not a good test because the databases themselves are rarely, if ever, blank. The solution that we advocate and have used on projects is to take a snapshot of the production database and run the programmer tests on the snapshot. This gives you a very good approximation of the actual database without having to worry about your tests messing up the production database.

By the end of this chapter, you should have a good understanding of the issues associated with writing programmer tests for databases and how some of the issues are mitigated using a combination of capabilities in the .NET Framework and some testing strategies presented here.

The Task

The first step is to brainstorm a list of tests that are needed for completion. The task overall is defined as building a read-only data access layer to support the retrieval of a *Recording* entity and all its associated entities. The existing database schema (described in Chapter 4) is shown in Figure 5-1.

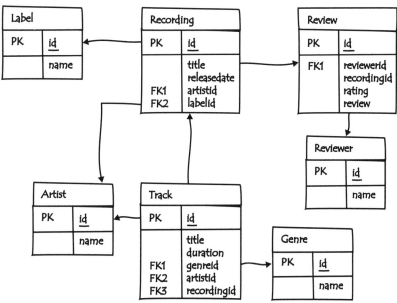

Figure 5-1   Recordings data model

So, given this schema and the task definition, what are the types of things we should test?

- Connecting to the database

- Individual entities in isolation (Recording, Label, Review, Reviewer, Track, Artist, and Genre)

- Relationships between entities (Review-Reviewer, Track-Genre, Track-Artist, Recording-Label, Recording-Reviews, Recording-Artist, Review-Recording, and Track-Recording)

- Retrieve a Recording and all its associated entities by specifying the recording id

The detail associated with this test list is much more typical than what was shown in Chapter 2, "Test-Driven Development in .NET—By Example." As we elaborate the solution, we will augment the list with more detail. Looking at the list, we have to be able to connect to the database to do anything, so we will begin by writing tests to connect to the database first.

Connecting to the Database

ADO.NET provides a set of classes to facilitate the database access, as well as several provider-specific packages that implement database access. Because our database is SQL Server 2000, we will use the SQL Server-specific provider that ships with the standard .NET framework distribution. Following is the code that establishes a database connection expressed as a test:

```
using System;
using System.Data;
using System.Data.SqlClient;
using NUnit.Framework;

[TestFixture]
public class SqlConnectionFixture
{
   [Test]
   public void ConnectionIsOpen()
   {
      SqlConnection connection =
         new SqlConnection(
            @"server=(local);database=catalog;Trusted_Connection=true");
      connection.Open();
      Assert.AreEqual(ConnectionState.Open, connection.State);
      connection.Close();
   }
}
```

Let's look at this test in detail. First, we construct a *SqlConnection* object by passing a connection string to the constructor; the syntax of this connection string is provider-specific, and in our example it contains the server information and the authentication method. Second, the database connection is not considered opened when it is constructed and needs to be opened explicitly. After the connection has been opened, we can verify its state by accessing the *State* property on the connection object; the *ConnectionState* enumeration defines the common connection states. When we finish with the connection, we use the *Close* method to close the connection.

> **Note**   With connection pooling in place, closing the connection does
> not actually tear down the established link to the database; the con-
> nection is simply returned to the pool, in which it stays opened until
> either it is requested by the application again or, after a period of being
> inactive, it is closed by the pool manager.

A Small Improvement

As you probably noticed, the connection string has hard-coded connection
information, which is environment-specific and should not be hard-coded in
the test or application code. There are a variety of ways to pass this information
to the application. One of the more common methods is to read the connection
string from a configuration file using the *ConfigurationSettings* class. Let's alter
the test code to use the configuration file:

```
using System;
using System.Configuration;
using System.Data;
using System.Data.SqlClient;
using NUnit.Framework;

[TestFixture]
public class SqlConnectionFixture
{
   [Test]
   public void ConnectionIsOpen()
   {
      string connectionString =
         ConfigurationSettings.AppSettings.Get("Catalog.Connection");
      Assert.IsNotNull(connectionString);

      SqlConnection connection =
         new SqlConnection(connectionString);
      connection.Open();
      Assert.AreEqual(ConnectionState.Open, connection.State);
      connection.Close();
   }
}
```

This test compiles, but it fails when we try to run it because we need to
create a configuration file that contains the connection string. For example

```
<?xml version="1.0" encoding="utf-8" ?>
<configuration>
   <appSettings>
```

```
    <add key="Catalog.Connection"
        value="server=(local);database=catalog;Trusted_Connection=true" />
    </appSettings>
</configuration>
```

An application configuration file can have many sections. In this example, we placed the connection string in the *appSettings* section. This section contains a collection of key-value pairs. We placed the connection property under the *Catalog.Connection* key.

When you are using NUnit and configuration files, the name of the configuration file must be the same as the name of the assembly with the .config suffix appended. For example, the assembly that contains the tests is named DataAccessLayer.dll. The name of the configuration file must be named Data-AccessLayer.dll.config and it must be placed in the same directory as the assembly itself for the NUnit executable to locate it.

We're Not Finished Yet

Looking at the test, you will notice that there are two unrelated assert methods: one to verify that a connection string is retrieved from the configuration file and the other to check whether we can open the connection. Because these two things test two different things, they should be separate tests.

Separating the Tests   We need to move the test that verifies that the connection string is read correctly from the configuration file into a new test. The following is the new test:

```
[Test]
public void CanRetrieveConnectionString()
{
    string connectionString =
        ConfigurationSettings.AppSettings.Get("Catalog.Connection");
    Assert.IsNotNull(connectionString);
}
```

Creating an additional test forces us to duplicate the retrieval of the connection string from the configuration file in each test. Therefore, we need to refactor the code so there is no duplication. We move the retrieval to a new method named *RetrieveConnectionString* and mark it with the *SetUp* attribute, which ensures that the connection string will be retrieved from the configuration file prior to each test being executed by NUnit. After we move the retrieval to the *RetrieveConnectionString* method, we need to modify the test methods to use it. Here is the code after the refactoring is completed:

```
[TestFixture]
public class SqlConnectionFixture
{
```

```
   private string connectionString;

   [SetUp]
   public void RetrieveConnectionString()
   {
      connectionString =
         ConfigurationSettings.AppSettings.Get("Catalog.Connection");
   }

   [Test]
   public void CanRetrieveConnectionString()
   {
      Assert.IsNotNull(connectionString);
   }

   [Test]
   public void ConnectionIsOpen()
   {
      SqlConnection connection =
         new SqlConnection(connectionString);
      connection.Open();
      Assert.AreEqual(ConnectionState.Open, connection.State);
      connection.Close();
   }
}
```

Now that we have established the connection to the database, we can move on to accessing the individual entities in the database.

Individual Entities in Isolation

The next item in the test list is to read individual entities from the database and check to see whether they are correct. To satisfy the need for executing the tests in a well-known state, we first have to insert an entity into the database, retrieve it, and then delete it after we are finished. We want to be able to look at each entity without having to create all the other entities, so we will use a typed *DataSet* to achieve this isolation. The following section describes how to construct a typed *DataSet* for the recording database.

Defining a Typed *DataSet* for the Recording Database

In this step, we will create a typed *DataSet* to capture our data schema. Because we are working with an existing database schema and we already know all the data tables and all the relationships between the entities, we will define the typed *DataSet* in one step instead of building it up incrementally. Figure 5-1 shows the relational data model we described in Chapter 4. The typed *DataSet*'s schema is defined and stored in an eXtensible Schema Definition (XSD) schema file. (A good discussion of XSD schemas can be found in *Essential XML Quick Reference* by Aaron Skonnard and Martin Gudgin.) The schema file can then be used by the xsd.exe tool to generate the code for the typed *DataSet* class.

The typed *DataSet* schema file can be produced either completely manually or with the help of the VisualStudio.NET DataSet Wizard. (There is a good discussion on how to create a typed *DataSet* in *Pragmatic ADO.NET*. We will not go into details of explaining how the wizard works, but will rather outline the process we went through to create the typed *DataSet* for the recording database.)

The Recording entity is central to the existing data model. It represents information about the recording and all its associated/dependent objects. We start by creating a blank *DataSet* named *RecordingDataSet*. The next step is to drag and drop the tables from the database server catalog onto the design palette. We then give meaningful names to the primary key columns for our tables. The wizard will create the tables using only the information available in the database schema; we can further refine the definition of our typed *DataSet* by annotating the elements with additional information about the data. The xsd.exe tool will understand and use these additional attributes when it generates the code. These additional attributes are defined in a special namespace: *urn:schemas-microsoft-com:xml-msprop*. Following is a fragment from the schema file that describes the Review table:

```
<xs:element name="Review" codegen:typedName="Review" codegen:typedPlu-
ral="Reviews">
   <xs:complexType>
     <xs:sequence>
        <xs:element name="id" type="xs:long" codegen:typedName="Id" />
        <xs:element name="reviewerid" type="xs:long" minOccurs="0" code-
gen:typedName="ReviewerId"/>
        <xs:element name="recordingid" type="xs:long" minOccurs="0" code-
gen:typedName="RecordingId"/>
        <xs:element name="rating" type="xs:int" codegen:typedName="Rating" />
        <xs:element name="review" type="xs:string" minOccurs="0" code-
gen:typedName="Content" />
     </xs:sequence>
   </xs:complexType>
</xs:element>
```

A few elements here need a bit more explanation:

■   The attribute *codegen:typedName="Review"* is an example of an annotation added to instruct the xsd.exe tool to use the name *"Review"* for a row of data in the typed *DataSet*.

■   The attribute *codegen:typedName="Id"* is used to define the name for the *id* property of the Review row. Without this attribute, the property would be called *"id"* (which violates a C# naming convention for properties—the names should begin with a capital letter).

■   The attribute *minOccurs="0"* on the review element indicates that this column allows null values in the database.

After the data tables are defined, we can add relationships. The relationships are not created automatically when we import the tables from the database—we need to do it manually. There are a couple of ways to define relationships between the tables: using key constraints or using unconstrained relationships. A *DataSet* object is designed to look and behave very similarly to the database, and the relationships in the database can be either enforced (using referential integrity constraints) or simply defined (using foreign key/primary key references). There are many benefits to enforcing the relationships in the database. (A high degree of data integrity is one of them.) However, enforcing the relationships in the typed *DataSet* makes the process of incremental code development very difficult because the objects are harder to isolate from their relationships. We want to be able to test individual objects in separation and then to test the relationship that exists between objects. For this reason, we decided not to enforce the relationships on the typed *DataSet* level and limit the referential integrity rules to the database. Because we will be writing plenty of tests to verify the correctness of the relationships between the objects in the typed *DataSet*, we will ensure that we do not break anything.

To define the relationships in our typed *DataSet* that are not enforced, we will use elements from the namespace *urn:schemas-microsoft-com:xml-msdata*. Following is an example of the relationship between the Recording and its Label:

```
<msdata:Relationship name="LabelOfTheRecording" msdata:parent="Label"
msdata:child="Recording" msdata:parentkey="id" msdata:childkey="labelid" />
```

After we have completed the definition of the schema for the typed *DataSet*, we can generate the code for the *RecordingDataSet*. VisualStudio.NET automatically runs the *DataSet* code-generation tool when the project is built. Now we're ready to write code that uses this typed *DataSet*.

Artist Gateway

Artist is the first database table we will work on. What we want to have is an object that contains all the SQL for accessing the *Artist* table. This includes selects, inserts, updates, and deletes. The rest of the code will call the methods in this object for all the interaction with this table. Encapsulating all the access into a single object is a common design pattern, which is called a *Table Data Gateway*. For more detailed information, see *Patterns of Enterprise Application Architecture*. The first test inserts a new *Artist* into the database with known values, retrieves the newly inserted *Artist*, and verifies that the data from the database matches the values that were used to create the entity.

Primary Key Management   In thinking about this test, we realize that we need to decide how to handle the primary keys for our data. There are several strategies to handle the primary keys for relational tables; the two most common ones are the following:

- Use an existing field that is unique (for example, use SSN as primary key for a person) or use a unique combination of existing fields (for example, a person's first name, last name, date, and place of birth).

- Use a synthetic primary key—this is the numeric column added to the table to serve as the primary key.

We will use synthetic primary keys because they are more efficient (indexing on a single numeric column is very fast and space-efficient), and our data model does not have a good candidate for native unique keys.

After we decide to use the synthetic primary keys, we need to decide how to generate them. Once again, there are several typical approaches:

- Use the database server facilities to manage primary key generation; most database servers have such capabilities, but they are all vendor-specific. For example, Oracle uses sequences for generation of unique ids, and SQL Server uses AutoIncrement columns.

- Let the application manage generation of the primary key values; this approach is more generic and allows possible implementations of different strategies for id generation.

We decided to go with the second option because we have an opportunity to better isolate our data objects from the database. We will be using a separate table, PKSequence, in the database to keep track of the ids for our data tables. This table has two columns:

- *tableName*   The name of the data table for which we keep the id.

- *nextid*   The value for the next id.

Having this separate table allows us to manage the range of ids for each data table. There is one downside to choosing this approach—we will need at least two trips to the database when we are inserting a new entity. The first trip is needed to retrieve the unique id. The second trip is to insert the record into the database. Even with this as a known issue, let's proceed with this strategy to see how it works out. Let's write the test now. Remember, it has to insert an *Artist* into the database, retrieve it and verify that it is correct, and then remove it.

ArtistFixture.cs

```
using System;
using System.Configuration;
using System.Data;
using System.Data.SqlClient;
using DataAccessLayer;
using NUnit.Framework;

[TestFixture]
public class ArtistFixture
{
    [Test]
    public void RetrieveArtistFromDatabase()
    {
        string artistName = "Artist";

        SqlConnection connection =
            new SqlConnection(
                ConfigurationSettings.AppSettings.Get(
"Catalog.Connection"));
        connection.Open();

        ArtistGateway gateway = new ArtistGateway(connection);
        long artistId =
            gateway.Insert(new RecordingDataSet(),artistName);

        RecordingDataSet loadedFromDB = new RecordingDataSet();
        RecordingDataSet.Artist loadedArtist =
            gateway.FindById(artistId, loadedFromDB);

        Assert.AreEqual(artistId,loadedArtist.Id);
        Assert.AreEqual(artistName, loadedArtist.Name);
        connection.Close();
    }
}
```

As you can see in the test code, the *ArtistGateway* is not responsible for establishing the connection or for the creation of the *RecordingDataSet*; the callers of the gateway are responsible for setting up these objects and passing them to the gateway. The reasoning is that we want to be able to control the lifetime of the *RecordingDataSet* that the gateway works with. In the test, we created two *RecordingDataSet* objects: one to create a new *Artist* and one to load an *Artist* from the database. We did not use the same *RecordingDataSet* object because we wanted to be sure that we actually loaded the new artist from the database and that we did not work with a cached in-memory version of it. As you will see, being able to control the *RecordingDataSet* outside of the gateway is important when we add relationships between objects. We also pass a connection object to the gateway because we want to be able to control the transactional boundaries outside of the gateway. For example, our test may want to roll back the transaction to undo the changes we made to the database. See Chapter 10 for a detailed description of working with transactions.

The following is the *ArtistGateway* implementation needed to support the first test:

```
using System;
using System.Data;
using System.Data.SqlClient;

namespace DataAccessLayer
{
    public class ArtistGateway
    {
        private SqlDataAdapter adapter;
        private SqlConnection connection;
        private SqlCommand command;
        private SqlCommandBuilder builder;

        public ArtistGateway(SqlConnection connection)
        {
            this.connection = connection;

            command = new SqlCommand(
                "select id, name from artist where id = @id",
                connection);
            command.Parameters.Add("@id",SqlDbType.BigInt);

            adapter = new SqlDataAdapter(command);
            builder = new SqlCommandBuilder(adapter);
        }

        public long Insert(
RecordingDataSet recordingDataSet, string artistName)
        {
            long artistId =
GetNextId(recordingDataSet.Artists.TableName);

            RecordingDataSet.Artist artistRow =
                recordingDataSet.Artists.NewArtist();
```

```
   artistRow.Id = artistId;
   artistRow.Name = artistName;
   recordingDataSet.Artists.AddArtist(artistRow);

   adapter.Update(recordingDataSet,
   recordingDataSet.Artists.TableName);

   return artistId;
}

public RecordingDataSet.Artist
   FindById(long artistId, RecordingDataSet recordingDataSet)
{
   command.Parameters["@id"].Value = artistId;
   adapter.Fill(recordingDataSet,
      recordingDataSet.Artists.TableName);
   DataRow[] rows = recordingDataSet.Artists.Select(
      String.Format("id={0}",artistId));

   if(rows.Length < 1) return null;
   return (RecordingDataSet.Artist)rows[0];
}

public long GetNextId(string tableName)
{
   SqlTransaction transaction =
      connection.BeginTransaction(
      IsolationLevel.Serializable, "GenerateId");

   SqlCommand selectCommand = new SqlCommand(
      "select nextId from PKSequence where tableName = @tableName",
         connection, transaction);
   selectCommand.Parameters.Add("@tableName",
      SqlDbType.VarChar).Value=tableName;

   long nextId = (long)selectCommand.ExecuteScalar();
   SqlCommand updateCommand = new SqlCommand(
   "update PKSequence set nextId = @nextId where tableName=@tableName",
      connection, transaction);
   updateCommand.Parameters.Add("@tableName",
      SqlDbType.VarChar).Value=tableName;
   updateCommand.Parameters.Add("@nextId",
      SqlDbType.BigInt).Value=nextId+1;
   updateCommand.ExecuteNonQuery();
   transaction.Commit();

   return nextId;
}
```

At first glance, you might think that is a lot of code for just one test. It is, we do not disagree, but there are two factors at play. The first is that conceptually we are testing one thing: the ability to retrieve an *Artist* from the database. The fact that we need all this code to do that is an issue, but it is not a big enough issue that we would want to split this up into multiple tests. Second, if the tests were more granular, we would be testing the ADO.NET API, which is something that we do not recommend. Let's drill down into the code to see what's really going on:

- The *Insert* method must be supplied with all the required data values so that all columns in the database that do not allow nulls can be set properly.

- The id field is required but is not supplied in the signature of the *Insert* method; because we decided to use the synthetic primary keys approach, the *Insert* method will generate a new key and return it after a new record is successfully created.

- The *FindById* method refreshes the data in the *RecordingDataSet* with data from the database by calling *Fill* on the *DataAdapter*.

- The *GetNextId* method does two database calls wrapped in one database transaction (*select* and *update*), which is necessary to ensure the data consistency. We will be talking more about concurrency and transactions in later chapters when we describe updating data.

The test runs and it is successful, but we decided to spot check the database and discovered that we did not clean up the database after the test was run. A brief examination of the test code reveals that we did not delete the artist that we inserted. As mentioned at the beginning of this chapter, testing code that has persistent side effects is harder because we have to remove the inserted entities explicitly. In this case, we have to provide the ability to delete an artist, even though we do not have a customer requirement. Let's modify the test to delete the inserted record. The change is in boldface in the following code:

```
[Test]
public void RetrieveArtistFromDatabase()
{
    string artistName = "Artist";

    SqlConnection connection =
        new SqlConnection(
            ConfigurationSettings.AppSettings.Get(
                "Catalog.Connection"));
    connection.Open();
```

```
ArtistGateway gateway = new ArtistGateway(connection);
long artistId =
  gateway.Insert(new RecordingDataSet(),artistName);

RecordingDataSet loadedFromDB = new RecordingDataSet();
RecordingDataSet.Artist loadedArtist =
  gateway.FindById(artistId, loadedFromDB);

Assert.AreEqual(artistId, loadedArtist.Id);
Assert.AreEqual(artistName, loadedArtist.Name);

gateway.Delete(loadedFromDB, artistId);
connection.Close();
}
```

The test calls a function on the *ArtistGateway* called *Delete* to remove the entity from the database. Here is the implementation:

```
public void Delete(RecordingDataSet recordingDataSet, long artistId)
{
  RecordingDataSet.Artist loadedArtist =
    FindById(artistId, recordingDataSet);

  loadedArtist.Delete();

  adapter.Update(recordingDataSet,
  recordingDataSet.Artists.TableName);
}
```

We compile and run the test, and it passes. We also looked at the *Artist* table in the database and verified that the test data was not left in the database. Let's now write a test that explicitly verifies that the *Delete* method works.

```
[Test]
public void DeleteArtistFromDatabase()
{
  string artistName = "Artist";

  SqlConnection connection =
    new SqlConnection(
    ConfigurationSettings.AppSettings.Get(
    "Catalog.Connection"));
  connection.Open();

  ArtistGateway gateway = new ArtistGateway(connection);
  long artistId =
    gateway.Insert(new RecordingDataSet(),artistName);
```

```
                 RecordingDataSet emptyDataSet = new RecordingDataSet();
                 long deletedArtistId =
                    gateway.Insert(emptyDataSet,"Deleted Artist");
                 gateway.Delete(emptyDataSet, deletedArtistId);

                 RecordingDataSet.Artist deletedArtist =
                    gateway.FindById(deletedArtistId, emptyDataSet);
                 Assert.IsNull(deletedArtist);
                 connection.Close();
              }
```

We compile and run the tests, and they both pass. Finally, we spot-check the database again just to make sure there are no leftover remnants. Before we move on to the next test, it looks like the test code has several code duplications, so it's time to refactor to remove the duplication. The duplications include the open and closing of the connection and the insertion of the test *Artist* into the database. We need to use the SetUp/TearDown capability of NUnit to remove this duplication. We will put the opening of the connection and the insertion of the test data into the *SetUp* method and the deletion of the test data and the closing of the connection into the *TearDown* method. We do this type of refactoring so often that we refer to it as a SetUp refactoring. Here is the *ArtistFixture* after the refactoring:

```
[TestFixture]
public class ArtistFixture
{
   private static readonly string artistName = "Artist";
   private SqlConnection connection;
   private ArtistGateway gateway;
   private RecordingDataSet recordingDataSet;
   private long artistId;

   [SetUp]
   public void SetUp()
   {
      connection = new SqlConnection(
         ConfigurationSettings.AppSettings.Get(
         "Catalog.Connection"));
      connection.Open();

      recordingDataSet = new RecordingDataSet();
      gateway = new ArtistGateway(connection);

      artistId = gateway.Insert(recordingDataSet,artistName);
   }
```

```
[TearDown]
public void TearDown()
{
   gateway.Delete(recordingDataSet, artistId);
   connection.Close();
}

[Test]
public void RetrieveArtistFromDatabase()
{
   RecordingDataSet loadedFromDB = new RecordingDataSet();
   RecordingDataSet.Artist loadedArtist =
      gateway.FindById(artistId, loadedFromDB);

   Assert.AreEqual(artistId,loadedArtist.Id);
   Assert.AreEqual(artistName, loadedArtist.Name);
}

[Test]
public void DeleteArtistFromDatabase()
{
   RecordingDataSet emptyDataSet = new RecordingDataSet();
   long deletedArtistId = gateway.Insert(emptyDataSet,"Deleted Artist");
   gateway.Delete(emptyDataSet,deletedArtistId);

   RecordingDataSet.Artist deletedArtist =
      gateway.FindById(deletedArtistId, emptyDataSet);
   Assert.IsNull(deletedArtist);
}
}
```

Now that we have tests to retrieve and delete an *Artist*, let's add a test to update an artist already in the database.

```
[Test]
public void UpdateArtistInDatabase()
{
   RecordingDataSet.Artist artist = recordingDataSet.Artists[0];
   artist.Name = "Modified Name";
   gateway.Update(recordingDataSet);

   RecordingDataSet updatedDataSet = new RecordingDataSet();
   RecordingDataSet.Artist updatedArtist =
   gateway.FindById(artistId, updatedDataSet);
   Assert.AreEqual("Modified Name", updatedArtist.Name);
}
```

This test specifies a new method in the *ArtistGateway* named *Update*, which needs to be added. The following is the implementation of *Update*:

```
public void Update(RecordingDataSet recordingDataSet)
{
    adapter.Update(recordingDataSet,
        recordingDataSet.Artists.TableName);
}
```

We compile the code and run the tests, and they all pass. Just because we are paranoid, we do check the database to make sure that we cleaned up correctly and there were no leftover test artists. That is all the work that we will do on the *Artist* table for now. Let's move on to the *Genre* table.

Genre Gateway

Let's write the same first test that we did for *Artist*. As you recall, we need to insert a *Genre* into the database, read it back, verify the contents, and then delete it. We will use the *ArtistFixture* code as a model because it is very likely that we will need to do similar tests for *Genre* that we did for *Artist*. Here is the *GenreFixture* with the *RetrieveGenreFromDatabase* test implemented:

```
[TestFixture]
public class GenreFixture
{
    private static readonly string genreName = "Rock";
    private SqlConnection connection;
    private GenreGateway gateway;
    private RecordingDataSet recordingDataSet;
    private long genreId;

    [SetUp]
    public void SetUp()
    {
        connection = new SqlConnection(
            ConfigurationSettings.AppSettings.Get(
            "Catalog.Connection"));
        connection.Open();

        recordingDataSet = new RecordingDataSet();
        gateway = new GenreGateway(connection);

        genreId = gateway.Insert(recordingDataSet, genreName);
    }

    [TearDown]
    public void TearDown()
    {
```

```
      gateway.Delete(recordingDataSet, genreId);
      connection.Close();
   }


   [Test]
   public void RetrieveGenreFromDatabase()
   {
      RecordingDataSet loadedFromDB = new RecordingDataSet();
      RecordingDataSet.Genre loadedGenre =
         gateway.FindById(genreId, loadedFromDB);

      Assert.AreEqual(genreId, loadedGenre.Id);
      Assert.AreEqual(genreName, loadedGenre.Name);
   }
}
```

In a similar fashion, we will use the code from *ArtistGateway* as a model for the *GenreGateway*. Here is the code that is needed for the first test:

```
public class GenreGateway
{
   private SqlDataAdapter adapter;
   private SqlConnection connection;
   private SqlCommand command;
   private SqlCommandBuilder builder;

   public GenreGateway(SqlConnection connection)
   {
      this.connection = connection;

      command = new SqlCommand(
         "select id, name from Genre where id = @id",
         connection);
      command.Parameters.Add("@id",SqlDbType.BigInt);

      adapter = new SqlDataAdapter(command);
      builder = new SqlCommandBuilder(adapter);
   }

   public long Insert(RecordingDataSet recordingDataSet,
string genreName)
   {
      long genreId = GetNextId(recordingDataSet.Genres.TableName);

      RecordingDataSet.Genre genreRow =
         recordingDataSet.Genres.NewGenre();
      genreRow.Id = genreId;
      genreRow.Name = genreName;
      recordingDataSet.Genres.AddGenre(genreRow);
```

```
        adapter.Update(recordingDataSet,
recordingDataSet.Genres.TableName);

        return genreId;
    }

    public RecordingDataSet.Genre
        FindById(long genreId, RecordingDataSet recordingDataSet)
    {
        command.Parameters["@id"].Value = genreId;
        adapter.Fill(recordingDataSet,
recordingDataSet.Genres.TableName);
        DataRow[] rows = recordingDataSet.Genres.Select(
            String.Format("id={0}",genreId));

        if(rows.Length < 1) return null;
        return (RecordingDataSet.Genre)rows[0];
    }

    public void Delete(RecordingDataSet recordingDataSet,
long genreId)
    {
        RecordingDataSet.Genre loadedGenre =
            FindById(genreId, recordingDataSet);
        loadedGenre.Delete();
        adapter.Update(recordingDataSet,
recordingDataSet.Genres.TableName);
    }

    public long GetNextId(string tableName)
    { /* same as in ArtistGateway */ }
}
```

There is some code duplication present in the *GenreGateway* as well as in the *GenreFixture*. The first and most obvious duplication is the *GetNextId* method, which is identical in the *GenreGateway* and the *ArtistGateway* classes. We need to move it out of the two gateway classes into something that can be shared between the two classes. The first step in the extraction is to write a test that tests the *GetNextId* method explicitly. We are putting this test in a separate fixture named *IdGeneratorFixture* because it is no longer logically part of the *ArtistFixture* or *GenreFixture*.

```
[TestFixture]
public class IdGeneratorFixture
{
    private SqlConnection connection;
```

```
[SetUp]
public void OpenConnection()
{
   connection = new SqlConnection(
      ConfigurationSettings.AppSettings.Get(
      "Catalog.Connection"));
   connection.Open();
}


[Test]
public void GetNextIdIncrement()
{
   SqlCommand sqlCommand = new SqlCommand(
      "select nextId from PKSequence where tableName=@tableName",
      connection);

   sqlCommand.Parameters.Add(
   "@tableName",SqlDbType.VarChar).Value="Artist";

   long nextId = (long)sqlCommand.ExecuteScalar();
   long nextIdFromGenerator =
   IdGenerator.GetNextId("Artist", connection);
   Assert.AreEqual(nextId, nextIdFromGenerator);
   nextId = (long)sqlCommand.ExecuteScalar();
   Assert.AreEqual(nextId, nextIdFromGenerator + 1);
}


[TearDown]
public void CloseConnection()
{
   connection.Close();
}
}
```

Now that we have a failing test, we can continue the process and extract the *GetNextId* method from the *GenreFixture* into its own class named *IdGenerator*.

```
public class IdGenerator
{
   public static long GetNextId(string tableName,
SqlConnection connection)
   {
      SqlTransaction transaction = connection.BeginTransaction(
IsolationLevel.Serializable, "GenerateId");

      SqlCommand selectCommand = new SqlCommand(
         "select nextId from PKSequence where tableName = @tableName",
```

```
        connection, transaction);
    selectCommand.Parameters.Add("@tableName",
        SqlDbType.VarChar).Value=tableName;

    long nextId = (long)selectCommand.ExecuteScalar();
    SqlCommand updateCommand = new SqlCommand(
        "update PKSequence set nextId = @nextId where tableName=@tableName",
        connection, transaction);
    updateCommand.Parameters.Add("@tableName", SqlDbType.VarChar).Value=table
Name;
    updateCommand.Parameters.Add("@nextId", SqlDbType.BigInt).Value=nextId+1;
    updateCommand.ExecuteNonQuery();
    transaction.Commit();
    return nextId;
    }
}
```

When we run this test, it passes, so we complete the refactoring by having the *ArtistFixture* and *GenreFixture* use this method directly. After the changes are made, we recompile the code and run all the tests again. They all succeed, so this refactoring is complete. Let's move on to the next duplication, which is in the test code.

If you examine the test code in *GenreFixture*, *ArtistFixture*, and *IdGeneratorFixture*, you will see that they all follow the same pattern. They all open a connection, do something specific to the type of fixture, and then close the connection. The best way to implement this solution is to create a common superclass that each of these fixtures would inherit from. The following is an abstract fixture that can be used to perform this function.

ConnectionFixture.cs

```
using System;
using System.Configuration;
using System.Data.SqlClient;
using NUnit.Framework;

[TestFixture]
public abstract class ConnectionFixture
{
    private SqlConnection connection;

    [TestFixtureSetUp]
    public void OpenConnection()
    {
        connection = new SqlConnection(
            ConfigurationSettings.AppSettings.Get("Catalog.Connection"));
        connection.Open();
```

```
    }

    [TestFixtureTearDown]
    public void CloseConnection()
    {
        connection.Close();
    }

    public SqlConnection Connection
    {
        get { return connection; }
    }
}
```

This fixture is meant to be inherited from to manage the connection to SqlServer for all the tests. It uses *TestFixture SetUp/TearDown* because the connection needs to be opened only one time for all the tests. This is different from *SetUp/TearDown*, which is executed prior to each test being run. The following code is the *IdGeneratorFixture*, which has been modified to use the *ConnectionFixture*. The SetUp/TearDown methods have been removed because they are now being handled in the *ConnectionFixture*. The rest of the changes are in boldface in the following code:

IdGeneratorFixture.cs

```
using System;
using System.Configuration;
using System.Data;
using System.Data.SqlClient;
using NUnit.Framework;
using DataAccessLayer;

[TestFixture]
public class IdGeneratorFixture : ConnectionFixture
{
    [Test]
    public void GetNextIdIncrement()
    {
        SqlCommand sqlCommand =
            new SqlCommand(
                "select nextId from PKSequence where tableName=@tableName",
                Connection);
        sqlCommand.Parameters.Add("@tableName",SqlDbType.VarChar).Value="Artist";

        long nextId = (long)sqlCommand.ExecuteScalar();
        long nextIdFromGenerator = IdGenerator.GetNextId("Artist", Connection);
        Assert.AreEqual(nextId, nextIdFromGenerator);
```

```
        nextId = (long)sqlCommand.ExecuteScalar();
        Assert.AreEqual(nextId, nextIdFromGenerator + 1);
    }
}
```

After reviewing the changes and making sure that all the tests pass, it seems as if we have removed the duplication. Let's finish up the tests for the *Genre*. We need to add a test for deletion and a test for update. They are very similar to the tests that were written for *Artist*, so they are not included here.

Finishing Up

Writing the tests and implementation for the rest of the tables—*Label*, *Reviewer*, *Review*, *Track*, and *Recording*—is very similar to what we have done for *Artist* and *Genre*. The only difference that we encountered was in testing updates; we chose to write a separate test for each field that we wanted to update instead of having one test that updates all the properties and then performs the verification. Once again, the point we are trying to get across with tests is isolation. We want each test to have only a single reason to change. Because the implementations did not provide any additional feedback into the design, they are left as an exercise to the reader.

Testing Relationships Between Entities

As was described previously, there is no enforcement of relationships in the typed *DataSet*. We made this decision to facilitate the separation of testing of individual entities from testing the relationships between entities. Without such separation, we would have to create an entire tree of related objects just to test one individual object in that tree. For example, if the relationship between the *Review* and *Reviewer* were enforced, we would have to create a *Reviewer* entity before we could test a *Review* entity, which would significantly complicate our test code. However, because the relationships are not enforced by the typed *DataSet*, we need to write tests to ensure that the relationships work as expected. We decided to organize these tests by having a separate test class for each relationship that exists in the schema. Because we are testing two related entities, we need to create both and build the relationship between the two after they are created. Let's begin by writing a test for the relationship between the Review and Reviewer entity.

ReviewReviewerFixture.cs

```
using DataAccessLayer;
using NUnit.Framework;
```

```
[TestFixture]
public class ReviewReviewerFixture : ConnectionFixture
{
    [Test]
    public void ReviewerId()
    {
        RecordingDataSet recordingDataSet = new RecordingDataSet();

        ReviewGateway reviewGateway = new ReviewGateway(Connection);
        long reviewId =
            reviewGateway.Insert(recordingDataSet, 1, "Review Content");

        ReviewerGateway reviewerGateway =
            new ReviewerGateway(Connection);
        long reviewerId =
            reviewerGateway.Insert(recordingDataSet, "Reviewer Name");

        RecordingDataSet.Review review =
            reviewGateway.FindById(reviewId, recordingDataSet);

        review.ReviewerId = reviewerId;
        reviewGateway.Update(recordingDataSet);

        Assert.AreEqual(reviewerId, review.Reviewer.Id);

        reviewGateway.Delete(recordingDataSet,reviewId);
        reviewerGateway.Delete(recordingDataSet,reviewerId);
    }
}
```

At first, the test inserts the two entities, *Review* and *Reviewer*, into the database. It then establishes the relationship between the entities. After the database is updated with the relationship, we test the ability to navigate from the *Review* to the *Reviewer* using the typed *DataSet*. After the test, we remove the test data from the database.

To complete the test list we need to write tests for the following relationships:

- Track-Genre

- Track-Artist

- Recording-Label

- Recording-Artist

- Recording-Reviews

- Review-Recording

We'll leave writing the tests for these relationships as an exercise for you because they are very similar to the *ReviewReviewerFixture* and they do not expose any additional design or implementation considerations.

Track-Recording Relationship

For the simpler entities such as *Artist*, it is simple to write the code to insert it into the database and remove it. That is not the case for *Recording*. The need to add the related objects significantly increases the amount of code that is needed to insert and remove the test data from the database. Because there is a lot of code and the need to have a test recording in multiple places, we will extract the insert/delete code from *RecordingGatewayFixture* and put it into its own class named *RecordingBuilder*.

```
using System;
using System.Data.SqlClient;
using DataAccessLayer;

public class RecordingBuilder
{
    private static readonly string title = "Title";
    private static readonly DateTime releaseDate =
        new DateTime(1999,1,12);

    private long recordingId;
    private long artistId;
    private long labelId;

    private RecordingGateway recordingGateway;
    private ArtistGateway artistGateway;
    private LabelGateway labelGateway;

    public RecordingDataSet Make(SqlConnection connection)
    {
        RecordingDataSet recordingDataSet = new RecordingDataSet();

        recordingGateway = new RecordingGateway(connection);
        artistGateway = new ArtistGateway(connection);
        labelGateway = new LabelGateway(connection);

        artistId = artistGateway.Insert(recordingDataSet, "Artist");
        labelId = labelGateway.Insert(recordingDataSet, "Label");
        recordingId = recordingGateway.Insert(recordingDataSet,title,
            releaseDate,artistId,labelId);

        recordingGateway.FindById(recordingId, recordingDataSet);
```

```
      return recordingDataSet;
   }

   public void Delete(RecordingDataSet dataSet)
   {
      artistGateway.Delete(dataSet,artistId);
      labelGateway.Delete(dataSet,labelId);
      recordingGateway.Delete(dataSet,recordingId);
   }

   #region properties
   public long LabelId
   { get { return labelId; } }

   public long ArtistId
   { get { return artistId; } }

   public string Title
   { get { return title; } }

   public DateTime ReleaseDate
   { get { return releaseDate; } }

   public long RecordingId
   { get { return recordingId; } }

   public RecordingGateway RecordingGateway
   { get { return recordingGateway; } }
   #endregion
}
```

Separating this class from the test code makes the creation of a test recording much simpler. Similar to what we did previously to share the database connection, we can also create an abstract class named *RecordingFixture* whose responsibility is to insert a *Recording* entity into the database upon the call to *SetUp* and delete the *Recording* entity when *TearDown* is called.

```
using DataAccessLayer;
using NUnit.Framework;
[TestFixture]
public abstract class RecordingFixture : ConnectionFixture
{
   private RecordingBuilder builder = new RecordingBuilder();
   private RecordingDataSet dataSet;
   private RecordingDataSet.Recording recording;

   [SetUp]
   public void SetUp()
```

```
    {
        dataSet = builder.Make(Connection);
        recording = dataSet.Recordings[0];
    }

    [TearDown]
    public void TearDown()
    { builder.Delete(dataSet); }

    public RecordingBuilder Builder
    { get { return builder; } }

    public RecordingDataSet.Recording Recording
    { get { return recording; } }

    public RecordingDataSet RecordingDataSet
    { get { return dataSet; } }
}
```

Finally, we will use the *RecordingFixture* in the *TrackRecordingFixture* to test the relationship between the *Track* and *Recording* entities:

```
using DataAccessLayer;
using NUnit.Framework;

[TestFixture]
public class TrackRecordingFixture : RecordingFixture
{
    private TrackGateway trackGateway;
    private long trackId;

    [SetUp]
    public new void SetUp()
    {
        base.SetUp();

        trackGateway = new TrackGateway(Connection);
        trackId = trackGateway.Insert(RecordingDataSet, "Track", 120);
        RecordingDataSet.Track track =
            trackGateway.FindById(trackId, RecordingDataSet);
        track.Recording = Recording;
        trackGateway.Update(RecordingDataSet);
    }

    [TearDown]
    public new void TearDown()
    {
        trackGateway.Delete(RecordingDataSet,trackId);
```

```
        base.TearDown();
    }

    [Test]
    public void Count()
    {
        Assert.AreEqual(1, Recording.GetTracks().Length);
    }

    [Test]
    public void ParentId()
    {
        foreach(RecordingDataSet.Track track in Recording.GetTracks())
        {
            Assert.AreEqual(Recording.Id, track.RecordingId);
        }
    }
}
```

This test verifies that for each track present you can navigate back to its associated recording. The tests pass, so we have completed the testing of the relationships. Looking at the test list, we have only the tests left that retrieve the *Recording* and all of its associated entities by specifying the recording id. Let's do that and finish up.

Retrieve a Recording

We need to write a test to retrieve a *Recording* with all the relationships filled in. We will call this method *FindByRecordingId*, and we will place this method in a class named *Catalog*. Just as in the previous tests, we need to insert a known recording and its associated entities into the database and then make the call to retrieve the recording and verify whether it is correct. After the tests are done, we then have to delete the known entity. We will use the *Recording-Builder* as we did previously to insert or delete a known recording. Here are the tests for the Catalog:

```
using System;
using DataAccessLayer;
using NUnit.Framework;

[TestFixture]
public class CatalogFixture : ConnectionFixture
{
// member variables …
    [SetUp]
```

```
public void SetUp()
{
   // code to insert the Recording entity …
   RecordingDataSet loadedDataSet = new RecordingDataSet();
   loadedRecording =
  Catalog.FindByRecordingId(loadedDataSet,recordingId);
}

[TearDown]
public void TearDown()
{ /* code to delete the Recording entity … */ }

[Test]
public void NotNull()
{ Assert.IsNotNull(loadedRecording); }

[Test]
public void CountTracks()
{
   RecordingDataSet.Track[] loadedTracks =
       loadedRecording.GetTracks();
   Assert.AreEqual(1, loadedTracks.Length);
}

[Test]
public void CountReviews()
{
   RecordingDataSet.Review[] loadedReviews =
       loadedRecording.GetReviews();
   Assert.AreEqual(1, loadedReviews.Length);
}

[Test]
public void ArtistOfTheRecording()
{
   RecordingDataSet.Artist loadedArtist = loadedRecording.Artist;
   Assert.AreEqual(artistId,loadedArtist.Id);
}

[Test]
public void LabelOfTheRecording()
{
   RecordingDataSet.Label loadedLabel = loadedRecording.Label;
   Assert.AreEqual(labelId,loadedLabel.Id);
}

[Test]
public void ArtistOfTheTrack()
```

```
   {
      RecordingDataSet.Artist loadedArtist =
         loadedRecording.GetTracks()[0].Artist;
      Assert.AreEqual(artistId,loadedArtist.Id);
   }

   [Test]
   public void GenreOfTheTrack()
   {
      RecordingDataSet.Genre loadedGenre =
         loadedRecording.GetTracks()[0].Genre;
      Assert.AreEqual(genreId,loadedGenre.Id);
   }

   [Test]
   public void ReviewerOfTheReview()
   {
      RecordingDataSet.Reviewer loadedReviewer =
         loadedRecording.GetReviews()[0].Reviewer;
      Assert.AreEqual(reviewerId, loadedReviewer.Id);
   }
}
```

These tests verify that we loaded the *Recording* from the database correctly. Given these tests, here is the implementation of *Catalog* that satisfies these tests:

```
using System;
using System.Configuration;
using System.Data;
using System.Data.SqlClient;
using DataAccessLayer;

public class Catalog
{
   public static RecordingDataSet.Recording FindByRecordingId(
      RecordingDataSet recordingDataSet, long recordingId)
   {
      SqlConnection connection = null;
      RecordingDataSet.Recording recording = null;

      try
      {
         connection = new SqlConnection(
            ConfigurationSettings.AppSettings.Get("Catalog.Connection"));
         connection.Open();
```

```
RecordingGateway recordingGateway = new RecordingGateway(connection);
recording = recordingGateway.FindById(recordingId, recordingDataSet);
if(recording != null)
{
    long artistId = recording.ArtistId;
    ArtistGateway artistGateway = new ArtistGateway(connection);
    RecordingDataSet.Artist artist =
        artistGateway.FindById(artistId, recordingDataSet);

    long labelId = recording.LabelId;
    LabelGateway labelGateway = new LabelGateway(connection);
    RecordingDataSet.Label label =
        labelGateway.FindById(labelId, recordingDataSet);

    GenreGateway genreGateway = new GenreGateway(connection);
    TrackGateway trackGateway = new TrackGateway(connection);
    foreach(RecordingDataSet.Track track in
        trackGateway.FindByRecordingId(recordingId, recordingDataSet))
    {
        artistId = track.ArtistId;
        long genreId = track.GenreId;
        artist = artistGateway.FindById(artistId, recordingDataSet);
        RecordingDataSet.Genre genre =
            genreGateway.FindById(genreId, recordingDataSet);
    }

    ReviewGateway reviewGateway = new ReviewGateway(connection);
    ReviewerGateway reviewerGateway = new ReviewerGateway(connection);
    foreach(RecordingDataSet.Review review in
        reviewGateway.FindByRecordingId(recordingId, recordingDataSet))
    {
        long reviewerId = review.ReviewerId;

        RecordingDataSet.Reviewer reviewer =
            reviewerGateway.FindById(reviewerId, recordingDataSet);
    }
}
finally
{
    if(connection != null)
        connection.Close();
}

return recording;
}
}
```

When you look at the implementation, it is clear that the *Catalog* code uses the gateway classes that we wrote earlier. If you look at the tests, you notice that the scope of the tests is somewhat different from the previous tests. They test the integration of all the gateways to load a *Recording* from the database. This would cause a problem if there were a failure in an underlying gateway that would cause these tests to fail as well. What you should strive for in your tests is to have a failure cause one and only one test to fail. This is often not possible, but it is a goal. If you can achieve this, your time in the debugger will be diminished because the failing test points you to the problem. In this case, we did not do that because we are testing the ability to load an object from the database. If we were to provide stub implementations of the gateway classes, we would not be using the database, so it does not seem like a worthwhile investment. The code compiles and all 45 tests pass and there are no tests left on the list, so let's do some housekeeping before we move on.

Test Organization

Now that we have tests for the data access layer, we can now look at the way our tests are organized. We have three categories in the test code: Entities, which test the entities in the database; Relationships, which test the relationships between entities; and Utilities, which test the supporting classes. The following is a detailed list of the fixtures in each category.

- Entities
  - ❏   *ArtistFixture*
  - ❏   *LabelFixture*
  - ❏   *ReviewerFixture*
  - ❏   *GenreFixture*
  - ❏   *ReviewFixture*
  - ❏   *TrackFixture*
  - ❏   *RecordingGatewayFixture*
- Relationships
  - ❏   *TrackGenreFixture*
  - ❏   *TrackRecordingFixture*
  - ❏   *TrackArtistFixture*
  - ❏   *ReviewReviewerFixture*

- ❏ *ReviewRecordingFixture*

- ❏ *RecordingArtistFixture*

- ❏ *RecordingLabelFixture*

- ❏ *RecordingReviewsFixture*

■ Utilities

- ❏ *IdGeneratorFixture*

- ❏ *SqlConnectionFixture*

The first step of organizing the tests is to separate the tests into a different assembly. This separation is done so it's easy to make the decision about whether to ship the tests or not when the software is deployed. The downside of this is that the tests must access only *public* classes and *public* methods. Given the way that we wrote the tests, this is not a problem with the code we have because the tests only access the public interfaces of the classes in the data access layer. However, there are times when you want to access internal members. In these cases, you can either leave your tests in the assembly or create what is called a multi-module assembly, with the tests in one module and the code in another. The reason this is not done more often is that the current version of Visual Studio.NET (VS.NET 2002 and 2003) does not support the creation of multi-module assemblies in C# or VB.NET, so you have to use command-line tools to build them.

After the test fixtures have been moved to a different assembly, you can also put them in namespaces associated with the categories they test: Entities, Relationships, and Utilities. This obviously is optional, but it serves a purpose to indicate to future readers what the intent was when the code was written, and it makes it easier inside NUnit to see which category is having trouble.

Summary

In this chapter, we have written the code for the data access layer to support the first feature. There were a number of issues that were uncovered as we explored the implementation. We chose to use a typed *DataSet*, which enabled us to test individual entities without having to create all the associated entities. The choice of the typed *DataSet* also allows us to be disconnected from the database, which has the promise of improved database connection utilization, but we will have to wait and see whether that is useful to our solution, and in fact it might be a detriment. Finally, what does it buy you to have these types of tests? The one thing that stands out is that the database schema is exactly what we are expecting. If the schema were to change, one or more of these tests would fail. Because the schema is not under our control, it is very useful to have a suite of tests to verify the external boundary. There are many questions still to be answered, so let's move on to the next chapter, in which we make the recording lookup functionality available as a Web service.

6

Programmer Tests: Using TDD with ASP.NET Web Services

In this chapter, we demonstrate how to write programmer tests when implementing a Web service in ASP.NET. To illustrate the issues, we will build on the functionality we implemented in Chapter 5, "Programmer Tests: Using TDD with ADO.NET" to provide a Web service interface to the recording database. By the end of this chapter, you should have an understanding of the issues involved in writing tests that have to execute inside ASP.NET, how to use the service interface pattern (see *Enterprise Solution Patterns in .NET* from Microsoft Corporation, 2003) to separate the protocol-specific aspects of the Web service from your application's functionality, and how to use stub classes to isolate portions of your application for improved testability.

The Task

The task is to implement a Web service that returns a Recording and all its associated entities (Tracks, Reviews, and so on) when specifying the "id" of the recording. The return type of the service needs to be in a format that is not dependent on the .NET Framework. The *Catalog* class that we implemented in the previous chapter returns a typed *DataSet* named *RecordingDataSet.Recording*, which is specific to the .NET Framework and directly coupled to the database schema. Therefore, we need to write some code that takes as input the typed *DataSet* and transforms it into a data structure that can interoperate with other systems.

A data structure like this is called a data transfer object[1] (DTO), which is one aspect of the Web service implementation. Another aspect is the communication protocol that exists between the provider of the service and the consumer. ASP.NET Web services provide the necessary plumbing to implement the communication protocol. The combination of the communication protocol and DTO is a design pattern called service interface. It is very useful to keep the service interface code separate from the rest of the application's functionality because the intent of the code is very different.

Test List

You need to complete the following tasks:

- Build an in-memory representation of a *RecordingDataSet*, map it into a DTO, and verify each field. This allows us to test the data transformation separate from the database and the Web service.

- Retrieve a *RecordingDataSet* from the database, map it into the DTO, and verify the fields. This is a partial integration test of the database and the service interface code. These tests are not dependent on the Web service.

- Retrieve a *RecordingDataSet* using the Web service interface and verify the fields. This will test the Web service in its entirety.

Why three different types of tests? We want to be able to use failing programmer tests to pinpoint a problem in the code. Because of the dependencies that exist in the code, it can be difficult to know where the problem is. We want to write our programmer tests in a way that minimizes the dependencies. For example, suppose that there is a failing programmer test in the Web service and no other failing tests. Because the problem manifests itself only in the Web service implementation, the problem is likely there. Having this isolation reduces the time spent debugging. The downside is that it will take some time and effort to achieve this isolation.

At the end of the chapter, we will review the overhead involved and let you be the judge about the value. For now, let's get started with the tests for data transformation.

---

1. Martin Fowler, *Patterns of Enterprise Application Architecture*, Boston: Addison-Wesley, 2003.

Data Transformation

The first step is to build a stub to isolate the Web service implementation from the data access code. We need a stub class because we want to hide how the *RecordingDataSet* is retrieved. The stub will return a *RecordingDataSet* that is built in-memory as opposed to one retrieved from the database. Here is the first test:

```
public class CatalogServiceStubFixture
{
   private RecordingDataSet.Recording recording;
   private RecordingDataSet.Recording actual;
   private CatalogServiceStub service;

   [SetUp]
   public void SetUp()
   {
      recording = CreateRecording();
      service = new CatalogServiceStub(recording);
      actual = service.FindByRecordingId(recording.Id);
   }

   private RecordingDataSet.Recording CreateRecording()
   {
      RecordingDataSet dataSet = new RecordingDataSet();

      RecordingDataSet.Recording recording =
         dataSet.Recordings.NewRecording();
      recording.Id = 1;

      /* more code to fill in the rest of the recording */

      return recording;
   }

   [Test]
   public void CheckId()
   {
      Assert.AreEqual(recording.Id, actual.Id);
   }
}
```

Given this test, here is the resulting *CatalogServiceStub* implementation:

```
public class CatalogServiceStub
{
   private RecordingDataSet.Recording recording;

   public CatalogServiceStub(RecordingDataSet.Recording recording)
```

```
    {
        this.recording = recording;
    }

    public RecordingDataSet.Recording FindByRecordingId(long id)
    {
        return recording;
    }
}
```

When we compile and run the test, it succeeds. Let's move on to the next test, which simulates an error condition.

```
[Test]
public void InvalidId()
{
    RecordingDataSet.Recording nullRecording =
        service.FindByRecordingId(2);
    Assert.IsNull(nullRecording, "should be null");
}
```

When we compile and run this test, it fails because the stub has no error-checking code contained in it. Does it make sense to put error-checking code in stub classes? Yes and no. Yes because it helps us explore what the real interface to a class might be with methods that return errors. No because you can get trapped into simulating very complex behavior for no apparent reason. We will simulate the error condition in the stub and we will see if the implementation is too complicated. Here's the code that makes the *InvalidId* test succeed:

```
public RecordingDataSet.Recording FindByRecordingId(long id)
{
    if(id != recording.Id) return null;
    return recording;
}
```

This code is certainly not too complicated, so it is probably all right to have this level of error-checking in this class. The tests pass, so let's turn our attention to the interoperability requirement.

Data Transfer Object

What should the DTO look like? We have a requirement to be platform-independent. We also have the need to hide the actual database schema from the clients. Lastly, we have to add some calculated fields, *totalRunTime* and *averageReview*, that are not present in the database. Figure 6-1 depicts the *RecordingDto*:

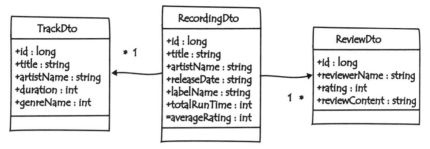

Figure 6-1   Data transfer object

In Figure 6-1, there are only three complex types defined in the schema: *RecordingDto*, *TrackDto*, and *ReviewDto*. When you look at the database schema, you see seven tables (Recording, Track, Review, Reviewer, Artist, Genre, and Label). We don't want to expose our client to the full complexity of the data model. (In a more realistic application, we could have hundreds of tables in the database schema, and many of them could be involved in a web of complex constrained relationships.) The reduction in complexity on the client side simplifies the mapping and the amount of data we need to move across the wire; in addition, the extra level of mapping allows us to customize the presentation of the data for particular client needs that also leads to data amount reduction. If you look again at Figure 6-1 and compare it to the data model for the typed *DataSet*, you notice the following differences:

- The *RecordingDto* has a flattened representation of label and artist information because we do not need to expose the data normalization artifacts on the client. (*ReviewDto* and *TrackDto* have similar simplifications for Reviewer, Artist, and Genre information.)

- There are two additional fields on *RecordingDto*: *totalRunTime* and *averageRating* (these fields are calculated).

- The type of *releaseDate* element on the *RecordingDto* is a string, not *DateTime* as it is on the *RecordingDataSet*; the client does not need the flexibility that the *DateTime* class provides because the client merely displays the data.

To specify this DTO in a platform-independent way, we write it using XML Schema. The Web Services Description Language (WSDL) specifies the use of XML Schema for maximum interoperability and platform neutrality. Here is Figure 6-1 expressed as an XML Schema:

Recording.xsd

```xml
<?xml version="1.0" encoding="utf-8" ?>
<xs:schema xmlns:tns="http://nunit.org/webservices" elementFormDefault="quali-
fied" targetNamespace="http://nunit.org/webservices" xmlns:xs="http://
www.w3.org/2001/XMLSchema">
<xs:element name="Recording" type="tns:RecordingDto" />
<xs:complexType name="RecordingDto">
   <xs:sequence>
      <xs:element minOccurs="1" maxOccurs="1" name="id" type="xs:long" />
      <xs:element minOccurs="1" maxOccurs="1" name="title" type="xs:string" />
      <xs:element minOccurs="1" maxOccurs="1" name="artistName"
        type="xs:string" />
      <xs:element minOccurs="1" maxOccurs="1" name="releaseDate"
        type="xs:string" />
      <xs:element minOccurs="1" maxOccurs="1" name="labelName"
        type="xs:string" />
      <xs:element minOccurs="0" maxOccurs="unbounded" name="tracks"
        type="tns:TrackDto" />
      <xs:element minOccurs="0" maxOccurs="unbounded" name="reviews"
        type="tns:ReviewDto" />
      <xs:element minOccurs="0" maxOccurs="1" name="totalRunTime"
        type="xs:int" />
      <xs:element minOccurs="0" maxOccurs="1" name="averageRating"
        type="xs:int" />
   </xs:sequence>
</xs:complexType>
<xs:complexType name="TrackDto">
   <xs:sequence>
      <xs:element minOccurs="1" maxOccurs="1" name="id" type="xs:long" />
      <xs:element minOccurs="1" maxOccurs="1" name="title" type="xs:string" />
      <xs:element minOccurs="1" maxOccurs="1" name="artistName"
        type="xs:string" />
      <xs:element minOccurs="1" maxOccurs="1" name="duration" type="xs:int" />
      <xs:element minOccurs="1" maxOccurs="1" name="genreName"
        type="xs:string" />
   </xs:sequence>
</xs:complexType>
<xs:complexType name="ReviewDto">
   <xs:sequence>
      <xs:element minOccurs="1" maxOccurs="1" name="id" type="xs:long" />
      <xs:element minOccurs="1" maxOccurs="1" name="reviewerName"
        type="xs:string" />
      <xs:element minOccurs="1" maxOccurs="1" name="rating" type="xs:int" />
      <xs:element minOccurs="1" maxOccurs="1" name="reviewContent"
        type="xs:string" />
   </xs:sequence>
</xs:complexType>
</xs:schema>
```

An additional benefit of using XML Schema is that we can generate C#
code from the XML Schema for use inside the program. We use the "xsd.exe"
tool to generate the code. Now that we have a DTO, we can modify the
CatalogServiceStub to return the DTO instead of a *RecordingDataSet*. The
changes to the *CatalogServiceStubFixture* are boldface in the following code:

```
private RecordingDataSet.Recording recording;
private RecordingDto dto;
private CatalogServiceStub service;

[SetUp]
public void SetUp()
{
    recording = CreateRecording();
    service = new CatalogServiceStub(recording);
    dto = service.FindByRecordingId(recording.Id);
}

[Test]
public void CheckId()
{
    Assert.AreEqual(recording.Id, dto.id);
}

[Test]
public void InvalidId()
{
    RecordingDto nullDto = service.FindByRecordingId(2);
    Assert.IsNull(nullDto, "should be null");
}
```

When we compile the modified tests, they fail because we did not change
CatalogServiceStub. Let's change that now.

```
public class CatalogServiceStub
{
    private RecordingDataSet.Recording recording;

    public CatalogServiceStub(RecordingDataSet.Recording recording)
    {
        this.recording = recording;
    }

    public RecordingDto FindByRecordingId(long id)
    {
        if(id != recording.Id) return null;
```

```
        RecordingDto dto = new RecordingDto();
        dto.id = recording.Id;
        return dto;
    }
}
```

Prior to this test, we returned a *RecordingDataSet.Recording*. Now that we have to return a *RecordingDto*, we need to map the fields from the *RecordingDataSet.Recording* into the *RecordingDto* in the *FindByRecordingId* method. This code is not in the right place because it seems as if it will be needed somewhere else. For now, let's leave it here, but we will definitely come back at some point and fix it. The code compiles and the tests pass, so let's move on to the rest of the fields.

Checking the "Title" Field

The next test is to verify the "title" field. Here is the *CheckTitle* test in the *CatalogServiceStubFixture*:

```
[Test]
public void CheckTitle()
{
    Assert.AreEqual(recording.Title, dto.title);
}
```

The test for title fails because we have not mapped the title field on *RecordingDto* yet. We need to make the following change to the *CatalogServiceStub*:

```
public RecordingDto FindByRecordingId(long id)
{
    if(id != recording.Id) return null;

    RecordingDto dto = new RecordingDto();
    dto.id = recording.Id;
    dto.title = recording.Title;
    return dto;
}
```

The test passes, and we can see the pattern for mapping the rest of the fields on the *RecordingDto*. As we mentioned previously, this code should not be in the stub because it will be needed by the service that talks to the database. So we need a place for this code that maps the *RecordingDataSet* into a *RecordingDto*. Martin Fowler refers to this concept as an Assembler.[2]

---

2. Martin Fowler, PEAA, page 405.

Building an Assembler

Both the Assembler and the *CatalogServiceStubFixture* have a need for an in-memory representation of the *RecordingDataSet.Recording*. The code to build that is contained in the *CatalogServiceStubFixture*, so we need to extract that code from there and put it in its own class so it can be shared. Let's create a new class called *InMemoryRecordingBuilder*, whose responsibility is to create in-memory recordings. Then we need to modify the *CatalogServiceStubFixture* to use the *InMemoryRecordingBuilder*. We run all the tests again to make sure that the refactoring did not break anything. The tests pass, so we can move on. The first test in the *RecordingAssemblerFixture* will be to verify that we can map the *id* field from the *RecordingDataSet.Recording* to the *RecordingDto*:

```
[TestFixture]
public class RecordingAssemblerFixture
{
    private RecordingDataSet.Recording recording;
    private RecordingDto dto;

    [SetUp]
    public void SetUp()
    {
        recording = InMemoryRecordingBuilder.Make();
        dto = RecordingAssembler.WriteDto(recording);
    }

    [Test]
    public void Id()
    {
        Assert.AreEqual(recording.Id, dto.id);
    }
}
```

This test code specifies that we need a class called *RecordingAssembler* to do the mapping from *RecordingDataSet.Recording* to the *RecordingDto*, and here is the implementation that satisfies the test:

```
public class RecordingAssembler
{
    public static RecordingDto
        WriteDto(RecordingDataSet.Recording recording)
    {
        RecordingDto dto = new RecordingDto();
        dto.id = recording.Id;
        return dto;
    }
}
```

Mapping of the *title, artistName,* and *labelName* are similar to the *id* field, so are not shown here in detail. The mapping of the *releaseDate* field brings up an interesting issue: the Assembler seems to not only map the data but also customize it for the specific presentation. For example, we chose to present the *DateTime* information on the client in the format "mm/dd/yyyy," and the Assembler does this transformation. It seems that the culture-specific *DateTime* formatting is the client's responsibility. We will leave it this way for now and check with the customer to see whether it is correct.

Mapping the Relationships in the Assembler

Now we have mapped all the fields of the *RecordingDto,* and we are ready to move on to the mapping of the related tracks and reviews. The first test will be to count the number of tracks that are associated with the Recording. Here's the test code:

```
[Test]
public void TrackCount()
{
    Assert.AreEqual(recording.GetTracks().Length,
dto.tracks.Length);
}
```

The test fails because we have not added the code for mapping tracks to the *RecordingAssembler.* We need to add the *WriteTracks* method to do the mapping:

```
private static void WriteTracks(RecordingDto recordingDto,
                    RecordingDataSet.Recording recording)
{
    recordingDto.tracks = new TrackDto[recording.GetTracks().Length];

    int index = 0;
    foreach(RecordingDataSet.Track track in recording.GetTracks())
    {
        recordingDto.tracks[index++] = new TrackDto();
    }
}
```

We will also modify the *WriteDto* method of the *RecordingAssembler* to call this method. Now the tracks are mapped on the *RecordingDto,* but the *TrackDtos* that we get on the recording are empty. We want to separate these two test fixtures: *RecordingDto* mapping is tested by *RecordingAssemblerFixture,* and *TrackDto* mapping is tested by *TrackAssemblerFixture.* To support the isolated testing of *TrackDto* mapping, we will introduce a new method on the *Recording-Assembler: WriteTrack.* This method takes a *RecordingDataSet.Track* and maps it to a *TrackDto*. Here is the code for the *TrackAssemblerFixture* with tests for all track fields:

```
[TestFixture]
public class TrackAssemblerFixture
{
    private RecordingDataSet.Artist artist;
    private RecordingDataSet.Genre genre;
    private RecordingDataSet.Track track;
    private TrackDto trackDto;

    [SetUp]
    public void SetUp()
    {
        RecordingDataSet recordingDataSet = new RecordingDataSet();

        artist = recordingDataSet.Artists.NewArtist();
        artist.Id = 1;
        artist.Name = "Artist";
        recordingDataSet.Artists.AddArtist(artist);

        genre = recordingDataSet.Genres.NewGenre();
        genre.Id = 1;
        genre.Name = "Genre";
        recordingDataSet.Genres.AddGenre(genre);

        track = recordingDataSet.Tracks.NewTrack();
        track.Id = 1;
        track.Title = "Track Title";
        track.Duration = 100;
        track.Genre = genre;
        track.Artist = artist;
        recordingDataSet.Tracks.AddTrack(track);

        trackDto = RecordingAssembler.WriteTrack(track);
    }

    [Test]
    public void Id()
    {
        Assert.AreEqual(track.Id, trackDto.id);
    }

    [Test]
    public void Title()
    {
        Assert.AreEqual(track.Title, trackDto.title);
    }
```

```
[Test]
public void Duration()
{
    Assert.AreEqual(track.Duration, trackDto.duration);
}

[Test]
public void GenreName()
{
    Assert.AreEqual(genre.Name, trackDto.genreName);
}

[Test]
public void ArtistName()
{
    Assert.AreEqual(artist.Name, trackDto.artistName);
}
}
```

Having added the tracks to the *RecordingDto*, we can write a test for the calculated field: *totalRunTime*. This field is the sum of the durations of all the tracks on the recording. The calculation of this field and the mapping are done on the *RecordingAssembler* by the *WriteTotalRunTime* method:

```
private static void WriteTotalRuntime(RecordingDto dto,
RecordingDataSet.Recording recording)
{
    int runTime = 0;
    foreach(RecordingDataSet.Track track in recording.GetTracks())
    {
        runTime += track.Duration;
    }
    dto.totalRunTime = runTime;
}
```

This method does not seem to fit with the rest of the mapping code (it feels out of place here), but we have not yet found a better place for it. Let's keep it here for awhile, but note it—both the *releaseDate* transformation and the *totalRunTime* calculations suggest that we need some other place for these "intelligent" mappings.

Mapping of relationships to Reviews is very similar to what we have done with the tracks, and we leave it as an exercise for the reader. The only interesting difference was the additional test we had to write to verify that if the recording does not have any reviews, the average rating is zero:

```
[Test]
public void AverageRatingZero()
```

```
{
    RecordingDataSet dataSet = new RecordingDataSet();

    RecordingDataSet.Recording recording =
        dataSet.Recordings.NewRecording();
    recording.Id = 1;
    recording.Title = "Title";
    recording.ReleaseDate = DateTime.Today;

    RecordingDataSet.Label label = dataSet.Labels.NewLabel();
    label.Id = 1;
    label.Name = "Label";
    dataSet.Labels.AddLabel(label);

    RecordingDataSet.Artist artist = dataSet.Artists.NewArtist();
    artist.Id = 1;
    artist.Name = "Artist";
    dataSet.Artists.AddArtist(artist);

    recording.Label = label;
    recording.Artist = artist;
    dataSet.Recordings.AddRecording(recording);

    RecordingDto dto = RecordingAssembler.WriteDto(recording);
    Assert.AreEqual(0, dto.averageRating);
}
```

After we finish with this test, all the code compiles and the tests pass, so we can now go back to the *CatalogServiceStub* and modify it to use the *Recording-Assembler*:

```
public RecordingDto FindByRecordingId(long id)
{
    if(id != recording.Id) return null;
    return RecordingAssembler.WriteDto(recording);
}
```

The code compiles, and we rerun all the tests. They all pass, so we can safely move on to the code that uses the database instead of the stub.

Database Catalog Service

In the previous section, we could isolate the tests and implementation from the database, which means that if we have a failing database test, it will not cascade into the tests for the *RecordingAssembler*. Now that we know that the code works in isolation, we need to hook up the code to the database so we can verify that the code on the server works correctly without the Web service. The first test is the *CheckId* test:

```
[TestFixture]
public class DatabaseCatalogServiceFixture : RecordingFixture
{
    private DatabaseCatalogService service;
    private RecordingDto dto;

    [SetUp]
    public new void SetUp()
    {
        base.SetUp();

        service = new DatabaseCatalogService();
        dto = service.FindByRecordingId(Recording.Id);
    }

    [Test]
    public void CheckId()
    {
        Assert.AreEqual(Recording.Id, dto.id);
    }
}
```

Although this code looks very similar to the *CatalogServiceStubFixture*, there are two big differences. First, the *DatabaseCatalogServiceFixture* inherits from *RecordingFixture* to insert Recording entities into the database. Second, we use a new class, *DatabaseCatalogService*, to retrieve the Recording from the database instead of using the *CatalogServiceStub*. Let's take a look at *Database-CatalogService*:

```
public class DatabaseCatalogService
{
    public RecordingDto FindByRecordingId(long id)
    {
        RecordingDataSet dataSet = new RecordingDataSet();
        RecordingDataSet.Recording recording =
            Catalog.FindByRecordingId(dataSet, id);

        if(recording == null) return null;
        return RecordingAssembler.WriteDto(recording);
    }
}
```

When we compile and run the test, it passes. However, there is a lot of duplication between the *CatalogServiceStub* and the *DatabaseCatalogService*. Let's refactor out the common parts into a base class called *CatalogService*:

```
public abstract class CatalogService
{
   public RecordingDto FindByRecordingId(long id)
   {
      RecordingDataSet.Recording recording = FindById(id);
      if(recording == null) return null;

      return RecordingAssembler.WriteDto(recording);
   }

   protected abstract
      RecordingDataSet.Recording FindById(long recordingId);
}
```

If you go back and look at the code for the *CatalogServiceStub* and the *DatabaseCatalogService*, the one thing that is different between them is the retrieval of the *RecordingDataSet.Recording*. The stub class creates the Recording in memory, and the database class retrieves it from the database. The *Catalog-Service* class uses an abstract method named *FindById* to allow derived classes to retrieve the Recording in the way that they see fit. Using the *CatalogService* base class, we can now modify the *CatalogServiceStub* to be the following:

```
public class StubCatalogService : CatalogService
{
   private RecordingDataSet.Recording recording;

   public StubCatalogService(RecordingDataSet.Recording recording)
   { this.recording = recording;}

   protected override
      RecordingDataSet.Recording FindById(long id)
   {
      if(id != recording.Id) return null;
      return recording;
   }
}
```

We did rename the class to be *StubCatalogService* because we like the naming convention we used with the *DatabaseCatalogService* better. The following is the modified *DatabaseCatalogService* class:

```
public class DatabaseCatalogService : CatalogService
{
   protected override
      RecordingDataSet.Recording FindById(long id)
   {
      RecordingDataSet dataSet = new RecordingDataSet();
```

```
            return Catalog.FindByRecordingId(dataSet, id);
        }
    }
```

We compile the code and rerun all our tests. They all pass, so we have successfully removed the duplication by introducing an abstract base class named *CatalogService* that now holds the common pieces of the code.

The rest of the tests in the *DatabaseCatalogServiceFixture* are similar to what we did for the stub. In fact, they are identical. This led us to believe that we could refactor them into one common base. It turns out that even though the tests are identical, the issues involved with different setup/teardown behavior are so noticeable and the code is so complicated that it did not make sense to refactor out the commonality right now.

Web Service Tests

Finally, we get to the point of hooking the whole thing up and using the functionality that we built previously through the Web service. The first test we will write is to verify the *id* field, just as we did previously with the stub and database versions. We will need a Recording inserted into the database just as we did with the database tests. Here is the first test:

```
[TestFixture]
public class CatalogGatewayFixture : RecordingFixture
{
    private CatalogGateway gateway = new CatalogGateway();
    private ServiceGateway.RecordingDto dto;

    [SetUp]
    public new void SetUp()
    {
        base.SetUp();
        dto = gateway.FindByRecordingId(Recording.Id);
    }

    [Test]
    public void Id()
    {
        Assert.AreEqual(Recording.Id, dto.id);
    }
}
```

As you can see, the tests do follow a similar pattern. We retrieve a *Recording-Dto,* in this case from a class named *CatalogGateway,* and verify that what was inserted into the database matches what is in the *RecordingDto*. Let's work on getting this to compile and run.

Web Service Producer and Consumer Infrastructure

Now, we need to address the question of how the test will access the Web service. We will use the "Add Web Reference" capability of Visual Studio .NET to generate the required code to handle the mechanics of consuming the Web service. But before we can create a Web reference, we need to define the Web service itself using WSDL. We will not author the WSDL by hand; we will once again rely on a tool to help us with the task.

We will use the WebMethod framework that comes as part of the ASP.NET Web services infrastructure. This framework allows generation of the required Web service WSDL by introspection of a class written in one of the .NET-supported languages. The framework defines a set of custom attributes that can be used to control the WSDL-generation process. Visual Studio .NET further simplifies the process of authoring a Web service by providing a Web service creation wizard that generates a template ASP.NET application to host the Web service. All we have to do is to define the code behind the page class that will implement the Web service's functionality.

Web Service Producer

We will name our Web service class *CatalogServiceInterface*. The wizard will generate the CatalogServiceInterface.aspx.cs template file, and we will add the *FindByRecordingId* WebMethod to this class:

```
[WebService(Namespace="http://nunit.org/services", Name="CatalogGateway")]
public class CatalogServiceInterface : System.Web.Services.WebService
{
    private DatabaseCatalogService service =
        new DatabaseCatalogService();

    public CatalogServiceInterface()
    {
        //CODEGEN: This call is required by the ASP.NET Web Services Designer
        InitializeComponent();
    }

    [WebMethod]
    public RecordingDto FindByRecordingId(long id)
    {
        return service.FindByRecordingId(id);
    }
}
```

The *CatalogServiceInterface* class uses the *DatabaseCatalogService* that we built previously for retrieval and transformation.

Web Service Consumer

Now that we have defined the WebMethod interface, we can generate the required code to consume the Web service. We will add a Web reference to our project by selecting the URL of the Web service to locate the WSDL of the Web service. The Web Reference Wizard takes care of the rest and generates the *CatalogGateway* proxy class that our client code can use to consume the Web service. The generated proxy supports both a synchronous and an asynchronous service consumption model, but in this example, we use only the synchronous communication mode.

Also, you may notice that the Web Reference Wizard generated a different *RecordingDto* class that is used as the type of the return value of the *FindBy-RecordingId* WebMethod on the client side. This is expected because the Web service consumer and producer can be built on two different platforms, and the consumer may have a different type of system. The Add Web Reference Wizard used only the information available in our WSDL file to generate the required client-side type mappings, and because the *RecordingDto* is not a primitive type directly supported by the Simple Object Access Protocol (SOAP) serialization, we ended up with two *RecordingDto* types—one on the server and one on the client. The Web services do not guarantee full type fidelity—this is the price we have to pay for interoperability.

Running the Test

Now we are ready to run the *CheckId* test in the *CatalogGatewayFixture*. We get a failure because the Web service does not have the database access connection properly configured. We will need to add the connection settings to the Web.config file. We run it again and we still have a failure; this time, the Web service was denied access to the database because we have not defined the proper database login name for the Web service.

Web Services Security

Security is one of the most important aspects of building distributed systems. Security for Web services is a very large subject, and its treatment is beyond the scope of this book. There are several specifications in progress that address the issues of Web services security on the SOAP messaging level.

We will briefly touch on some of the security-integration aspects to the extent necessary to proceed with our work. We will consider the Web services security only as it is supported by the existing HTTP transport infrastructure. Because ASP.NET Web services are hosted as typical ASP.NET applications, the existing ASP.NET security infrastructure for authentication and authorization can be reused for Web services. We will need to decide how to manage the security context propagation from the ASP.NET tier to the ADO.NET tier of our application. We have a couple of options here:

■ **Direct security context propagation by using trusted connections to the database**   Using this approach requires creating database login accounts for the ASP.NET user principals. If we support anonymous access to the ASP.NET application hosting our Web service, we will need to create an ASPNET account in the database server and grant this account the proper access rights to our catalog. If the ASP.NET application requires proper user authentication for access to the Web service, we may need to create several database accounts for each authenticated user principal. One of the main advantages of this approach is the fact that we can reuse existing database server security infrastructure to protect access to the data; however, this approach will also lead to the creation of individual connection pools for each user principal, and it does not scale well for a large number of users.

■ **Mapped security contexts**   In this approach, we will have a single database login account for the entire Web service application. We can do either of the following:

❑ Explicitly pass the user credentials to the database server for authentication (the username and password for this database login account will be stored in the Web.config file).

❑ Map the caller principal on the ASP.NET service thread to the desired database login name and use the trusted connection to the database.

The mapped security context approach does not require creating a large number of connections (one for each distinct user principal).

We will be using the direct security context propagation approach and allow anonymous access to the Web service application to avoid creation of multiple database connections. Following this decision, we will need to add the ASP.NET user to the list of database login accounts and grant read/write rights for the catalog schema to this account. After making this change, we are ready to run our test again. Now it passes, and we are ready to move on and write the rest of the tests.

The tests for most of the fields were the same, but the tests *TrackCount* and *ReviewCount* were slightly different. In *DatabaseCatalogService* and in

StubCatalogService, we could get the number of tracks or reviews by calling the *Length* method on the tracks and reviews fields, respectively. When we tried this on the Web service tests, we got a null reference exception. It turns out that if there are no tracks or reviews, the fields are not initialized as empty arrays—they are left only as *null* values. So we had to change the tests on the *Catalog-GatewayFixture* to the following:

```
[Test]
public void TrackCount()
{
    Assert.AreEqual(0, Recording.GetTracks().Length);
    Assert.IsNull(dto.tracks);
}
[Test]
public void ReviewCount()
{
    Assert.AreEqual(0, Recording.GetReviews().Length);
    Assert.IsNull(dto.reviews);
}
```

After we made these changes, we recompiled the code and reran all three sets of tests. They all pass, so we are done with the tests for the functionality. One last time we revisited the commonality of the *CatalogGatewayFixture*, *Database-CatalogServiceFixture*, and *StubCatalogServiceFixture*, and again we could not come up with anything that reduced the code duplication and increased the communication of what we were trying to do. So, this is one of those cases where there is code duplication but removing it reduces the communication.

Almost Done

One last thing we will do here is clean up some of the dependencies we have introduced. Our package structure has emerged as we were building up the Web service and integrating it with the data access. We have enough code written now to help us see the dependencies between the modules. We will be moving the classes around between assemblies and namespaces to better reflect the emerged architecture. This is an important step of the test-driven development process; we are in fact exposing our architecture by clarifying the packaging boundaries.

We want to be able to distribute our production code without our test code, which necessitates the separation of the service interface tests into a separate assembly just as we did in the previous chapter with the data access tests. The second restructuring we want to do is move the definition of the typed *DataSet*, *RecordingDataSet* into a separate assembly and into a separate namespace: *DataModel*.

Figure 6-2 represents the emerged architectural packages.

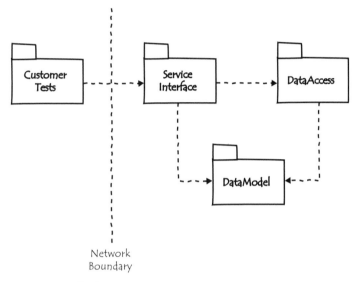

Figure 6-2   Package structure

The Bad News

Unfortunately, manual refactoring of the code of this scope is quite difficult and can be time-consuming; however, it is no less important. Of course, the tests give us the confidence that after the refactoring everything still works, but the process of moving classes between namespaces and assemblies is not as simple as it could have been if there were tools that better supported such activity. The process is not complicated—in fact, it is very mechanical and repeatable; but when we have many classes to move around, it quickly becomes annoying. The build process and the source control system also lag in support of such activity. This is not some fundamental limitation of the approach; it is the lack of adequate tool support that makes it harder.

Summary

When you look over the implementation, a number of things stand out. We use a common design pattern named service interface to separate the aspects of the Web service from the rest of the application's functionality. We introduced a stub class to separate the logical functionality from the database and the Web service. This stub allows us to work on the logical functionality without having to worry about the complications that the database and the Web service add to the problem.

For interoperability purposes, we developed a DTO, defined in XML Schema, to ensure the maximum amount of interoperability for the return type of the Web service.

Emerging Architecture

We have written a set of both integration and isolation unit tests. Having built a substantial portion of our application infrastructure, we started to recognize the emerging application architecture. Seeing the coupling between the classes and test code made it easier to recognize the packaging boundaries. We have refactored our application structure to reflect the emerging architecture.

7

Customer Tests: Completing the First Feature

In this chapter, we develop a set of customer tests for retrieving recording information via the Web service we wrote in the previous chapter. The intent of the customer tests is different from that of the programmer tests. Customer tests confirm how the feature is supposed to work as experienced by the end user. Because most customers might not feel comfortable coding their tests in NUnit, we need to provide a tool that makes writing tests as easy as editing a document. The goal is to enable the customer to write a specification as a series of automated tests. The tool that we will use to facilitate the automation of customer tests is an open-source tool called FIT. You can download it from *http://fit.c2.com*.

Are We Done?

This is an age-old problem in software development: many times, we have been on projects in which we thought we were 80 or 90 percent complete, only to have it take much more time than we thought it would to complete the last 10 or 20 percent. One of the main reasons for this problem is having ambiguous or contradictory requirements. We don't mean to imply that requirements in general are poorly written—only that when things are written down by people and read by other people, there will be different interpretations of what is written. These different interpretations can lead you to believe that you are finished when you are not.

So, how do you drive ambiguity out of this process? Clearly, during the writing of the software, we used programmer tests to ensure that various programming-related assumptions were correct. However, the scope of these tests is such that they could be written perfectly with 100-percent coverage and still could miss a critical function. So, this is a necessary step, but it is not sufficient to indicate completion. Although we also worked very hard to eliminate code duplication in the implementation, this duplication issue is not something that the customer is primarily concerned with, at least at the start.

Programmer tests and good software structure are useful metrics from the programming perspective because they give the programmers an indication of how well the software implements its intended functionality. It is really up to the customer to indicate whether the software serves its intended purpose because he is primarily concerned with what the software does and how this particular functionality relates to a business value. So, the determination of completion is related to these values. What is lacking in many cases is a means for the customer to indicate with precision whether or not the software works as it was expected to.

Customer Tests

What is needed then is a mechanism for the customer to write tests that are used to determine completion. These tests are a direct interpretation of the requirements, but they are written by the customer to ensure that their perspective is verified. Therefore, these tests should be in a form that is familiar to the customer, so this leaves out tests implemented with NUnit because most customers won't want to (or can't) write tests in a programming language.

Also, to facilitate the type of feedback that we get from programmer tests, these customer tests need to be automated to enhance reliability and improve response time. Rapid response time allows the development team to better associate a failure with the code change that caused it. For example, let's say it takes two weeks to run acceptance tests and get the results. Because it takes two weeks to do so, we will not do this very often. In fact, we will build up a list of changes to make the most appropriate usage of the testing resources. In addition, the development keeps moving when the tests are being run, so the software could be very different when the results are returned. If there were problems, the development team must now attempt to fix them. Some of the problems may have already been fixed; some may no longer be reproducible, and so on. For the sake of argument, let's say that it takes five minutes to run the customer tests and get the results. This time is so short that you want to add running these tests in addition to the programmer tests for each build of the software. Given this immediate feedback when a test fails, it is much more likely that the person who made the change in the software can go back and fix it without a great deal of time spent wondering what caused the problem. This rapid turnaround yields very large productivity gains for the team.

Customer Tests for Recording Retrieval

The first feature implemented provides a way to retrieve a recording's information via a Web service. Given this statement, the programmers wrote an implementation to satisfy this requirement. Now that the implementation is complete, we need a set of tests from the customer perspective to verify that the implementation does what the customer expects.

The first step is to develop a script to test the implementation manually. (I know we said that this was not desirable, but before we can automate something we have to know what it is.) The following are two samples of the test scripts:

Script 1. Retrieve an existing recording and verify its content

1. Retrieve a recording with an id of 4 via the Web service.
2. Verify that the recording's title is "The Rising".
3. Verify that the artist's name is "Bruce Springsteen".
4. Verify that the release date is "7/30/2002".
5. Verify that the recording's duration is "72:51".
6. Verify that the label name is "Sony".
7. Verify that the track 1 title is "Lonesome Day".
8. Verify that the track 1 artist's name is "Bruce Springsteen".
9. Verify that the track 1 genre is "Rock".
10. Verify that the track 1 duration is "4:08".

Steps 11 through 56 are not shown here. These steps verify the rest of the track information for the remaining tracks and are similar to steps 7 through 10.

57. Verify that the average recording's rating is "4".
58. Verify that the review 1 reviewer name is "Bob".
59. Verify that the review 1 review content is "I thought it was great".
60. Verify that the review 1 rating is "5".

There are additional steps for each review present, and they are similar to 58 through 60.

Script 2. Retrieve a nonexistent recording

1. Retrieve a recording with an id of 100002 via the Web service.
   This id is not currently assigned to any recording and should not be.

2. Verify that the recording was not found.

There are several other scripts written that are similar to the ones shown; these additional scripts verify information about other existing recordings in the database.

Because we have not implemented a UI, one way to "run" these scripts is to use the ASP.NET Web service infrastructure to exercise the Web service.

The customer will point the Internet Explorer browser to the URL of our Web service. Figure 7-1 shows a sample of the page that they see.

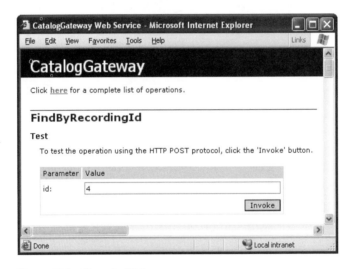

Figure 7-1 Sample Web page

The customer enters the id of "4" and presses the Invoke button. The response that he receives is an XML document with the data about the recording returned by the Web service. A fragment of this XML document is shown here:

```
<?xml version="1.0" encoding="utf-8"?>
<Recording xmlns:xsd="http://www.w3.org/2001/XMLSchema" xmlns:xsi="http://
www.w3.org/2001/XMLSchema-instance" xmlns="http://nunit.org/webservices">
  <id>4</id>
```

```
<title>The Rising</title>
<artistName>Bruce Springsteen</artistName>
<releaseDate>7/30/2002</releaseDate>
<labelName>Sony</labelName>
<tracks>
  <id>45</id>
  <title>Lonesome Day</title>
  <artistName>Bruce Springsteen</artistName>
  <duration>248</duration>
  <genreName>Rock</genreName>
</tracks>
… the rest of the information
</Recording>
```

The customer has to manually verify each field in the XML. For example, for the recording's title, the user will locate the *<title>…</title>* tag of the *<Recording>* element and verify that the content of this tag is *The Rising*. (All you have to do is try the first script, which is longer than 60 steps, and you start to realize how long, tedious, and boring this is.) A single test takes several minutes and runs only when the customer has time to do it. Therefore, we should not expect the customer to be willing to perform these tests frequently and to do them when we need them done.

These test scripts are calling out for some form of automation. In fact, computers are very good at comparing two things, so let's automate these tests so they can be performed when they are needed and be less error-prone.

Automating Customer Tests

Although many tools can be used to perform test automation, we will focus our attention on FIT, which seems very well-suited to perform the tests we need.

FIT Overview

FIT uses HTML tables to structure customer tests. For example, the following table is a sample customer test for dividing numbers from the FIT Web site:

eg.Division		
numerator	denominator	quotient()
1000	10	100.0000
-1000	10	-100.0000

eg.Division		
numerator	**denominator**	**quotient()**
1000	7	142.85715
1000	.00001	100000000
4195835	3145729	1.3338196

The way to interpret this table (let's ignore the first two rows for a moment) is to read each row as a separate test. The first two columns are input to the software, and the third column is the expected result, in this case. The first row verifies the equation (1000/10 = 100.0000). So, even without understanding how FIT does what it does, you can read and understand the tests. You also do not need to know how FIT runs the test. When FIT runs the script, you get the following result:

eg.Division		
numerator	**denominator**	**quotient()**
1000	10	100.0000
-1000	10	-100.0000
1000	7	142.85715
1000	.00001	100000000
4195835	3145729	1.3338196

As part of the running of the script, the code is exercised and the verification is performed. In this case, all the tests pass, so all the cells in the quotient() column are shaded, indicating success. If there is a failure, the table cell is colored red and the actual value is present along with the expected value, which allows the customer to look through the tests at a glance and see the tests that pass and the ones that don't. (If this were a four-color book, you'd see the green shade of a cell for success and red for failure in the tables on this page.) Also, because this is HTML you can add additional content that explains what is being tested around the tests (which can be text or graphics). This content turns these HTML documents into the form of an executable specification.

Connecting FIT to the Implementation

To be able to specify your tests in this manner, you need a bridge between the FIT framework and your software. In the previous table, the first row specifies a class, *eg.Division*, which is used as the bridge between FIT and the actual implementation. The second row specifies methods that are called on the *eg.Division* class that FIT calls during the execution of the test. In the next section, we describe in detail how you can take the manual script from the previous section and convert it into an automated script run by FIT using our Web service.

Automation with FIT

The first step in the script is to verify that we can retrieve a recording given its id. Following is the translation of the manual step into the format of the table to be used in FIT.

fit.ActionFixture		
start	CustomerTests.CatalogAdapter	
enter	FindByRecordingId	4
check	Found	true

This test uses a class contained in the FIT framework named *ActionFixture*, which is a simple controller that parses each row and passes the values off to the appropriate handler. The header of the table defines the controller used to run the test. Each subsequent row in the table defines a step in the script. This test script uses the *start*, *enter*, and *check* commands that are part of the *ActionFixture*.

Start Command

The *start* step has a special meaning: it is used to initialize a class that is used to adapt the application classes to run inside the FIT framework. In this example, the name of this special class is *CustomerTests.CatalogAdapter*, which has to be written to support running the FIT tests and should not be considered a part of the application itself. Because it is strictly for FIT integration, it should not contain any application-specific logic beyond that needed to test.

Enter Action

The next row in the table begins with the *enter action*. This step is a simple action to be taken against the application via the adapter. In this case, the script specifies that the application must call the *FindByRecordingId* method on the *CatalogAdapter* to retrieve a recording with the recording id equal to 4. This method will change the state of the *CatalogAdapter* so that the retrieved recording is available for further steps.

Check Action

The last row in the table begins with the *check action*, which is the verification of the correctness of the application's response to previous user input. There are two parts to each check operation:

- **What to check** This is the name of the method defined on the adapter to use for application response verification. In our example, we want to verify that the recording is correctly retrieved; our *CatalogAdapter* class defines a *Found* method that can be called to verify that the recording is successfully retrieved.

- **What value the user expects to receive from the application** In our example, we expect the *Found* method to return *True* to indicate that the recording with the given recording id is found.

CatalogAdapter

The test script shown previously specified a class named *CatalogAdapter*. Its job is to adapt the calls that FIT will make into the actual calls to the Web service.

```
namespace CustomerTests
{
    public class CatalogAdapter : Fixture
    {
        private CatalogGateway gateway = new CatalogGateway();
        private static RecordingDto recording;

        public void FindByRecordingId(long id)
        {
            recording = gateway.FindByRecordingId(id);
        }

        public bool Found()
        {
            return recording != null;
        }
    }
}
```

This class seems to fit the requirement in that it simply adapts our existing software to the FIT framework. Notice that the names of the methods have to match the names specified in the test script. Otherwise, the test results will show exceptions for these rows.

Running the Script

We use the *FileRunner* class in FIT to run the test script. Figure 7-2 demonstrates the sequence of messages exchanged between FIT, the *CatalogAdapter*, and the Web service during the execution of the test script:

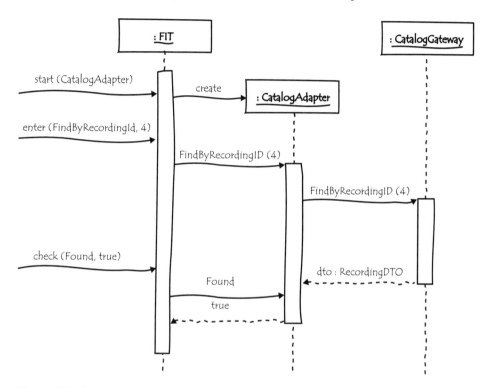

Figure 7-2   Message exchange

Running this test yields the following result:

fit.ActionFixture		
start	CustomerTests.CatalogAdapter	
enter	FindByRecordingId	4
check	Found	true

In addition, FIT provides a test summary section that gives statistics related to the execution of the test script, as you see at the top of the next page:

fit.Summary	
run elapsed time	0:00.94
run date	12/30/2003 12:15:39 PM
output file	CatalogResult.html
input update	12/30/2003 11:53:30 AM
input file	CatalogTest.html
fixture path	.;build;build\bin;obj;bin;bin\Debug;bin\Release;C:\book-example\v2\ fit.runner\bin\Debug
counts	1 right, 0 wrong, 0 ignored, 0 exceptions

Continuing with the Automation

Now that we can retrieve recordings from the database using FIT scripts, we need to augment the script to also check the content of the recording.

Fit.ActionFixture		
start	CustomerTests.CatalogAdapter	
enter	FindByRecordingId	4
check	Title	The Rising
check	ArtistName	Bruce Springsteen
check	ReleaseDate	7/30/2002
check	LabelName	Sony
check	Duration	72:51

This script is very much like the previous one. To get this script to work, we have added the following methods to the *CatalogAdapter*: *ArtistName*, *Release-Date*, *LabelName*, and *Duration*. These methods simply return the appropriate value from the *RecordingDto* object that is retrieved by the *enter action*. The modifications result in the following changes to the *CatalogAdapter*:

```
namespace CustomerTests
{
    public class CatalogAdapter : Fixture
    {
        private CatalogGateway gateway = new CatalogGateway();
        private static RecordingDto recording;
```

```
public void FindByRecordingId(long id)
{
   recording = gateway.FindByRecordingId(id);
}

public bool Found()
{
   return recording != null;
}

public string Title()
{
   return recording.title;
}

public string ArtistName()
{
   return recording.artistName;
}

public string ReleaseDate()
{
   return recording.releaseDate;
}

public string LabelName()
{
   return recording.labelName;
}

public string Duration()
{
   return recording.totalRunTime.ToString();
}
   }
}
```

The adapter maintains its rather mundane existence. The only thing of interest or concern is that the type of the *Duration* implies a data conversion from an integer to a string. This situation seems odd, and in fact when we run the test we get the following result:

fit.ActionFixture		
start	CustomerTests.CatalogAdapter	
enter	FindByRecordingId	4

fit.ActionFixture		
check	Title	The Rising
check	ArtistName	Bruce Springsteen
check	ReleaseDate	7/30/2002
check	LabelName	Sony
check	Duration	72:51 expected
		4371 actual

There is a failure. The *Duration* specified in the test script was 72:51, but the number we get back from the adapter is 4371. This is clearly a problem that will need to be addressed. For now, though, let's continue with the rest of the conversion process, and we promise to come back later and correct this problem. There is no way we can forget because every time we run the test it fails.

Verifying Track Information

The next part in the manual script verifies track information. It turns out that FIT has a different type of fixture, a *RowFixture,* that works best for this type of test. From the FIT website: "A *RowFixture* compares rows in the test data to objects in the system under test. Methods are invoked on the objects and returned values compared to those in the table. An algorithm matches rows with objects based on one or more keys. Objects may be missing or in surplus and are so noted." This type of fixture fits very well with looking for track information associated with a particular recording. The Track tests from the manual test script expressed in a *RowFixture* looks like this:

CustomerTests.TrackDisplay			
Title()	**ArtistName()**	**GenreName()**	**Duration()**
Lonesome Day	Bruce Springsteen	Rock	4:08
Into The Fire	Bruce Springsteen	Rock	5:04
Waitin' On A Sunny Day	Bruce Springsteen	Rock	4:18
The Nothing Man	Bruce Springsteen	Rock	4:23
Let's Be Friends	Bruce Springsteen	Rock	4:21
The Fuse	Bruce Springsteen	Rock	5:37
Further On (Up The Road)	Bruce Springsteen	Rock	3:52
Mary's Place	Bruce Springsteen	Rock	6:03

CustomerTests.TrackDisplay			
Title()	**ArtistName()**	**GenreName()**	**Duration()**
The Rising	Bruce Springsteen	Rock	4:50
My City Of Ruins	Bruce Springsteen	Rock	5:00
Empty Sky	Bruce Springsteen	Rock	3:34
Worlds Apart	Bruce Springsteen	Rock	6:07
Paradise	Bruce Springsteen	Rock	5:39
You're Missing	Bruce Springsteen	Rock	5:11
Countin' On A Miracle	Bruce Springsteen	Rock	4:24

This takes a bit of explanation. We need to implement another adapter that inherits from *RowFixture* to retrieve track information from the recording. Unfortunately, this script does not stand alone; it requires that a recording was retrieved in a previous step. In this case, the script will be run after the previous one. The *TrackDisplay* class is shown as follows:

```
public class TrackDisplay : RowFixture
{
    protected override Type getTargetClass()
    {
        return typeof(CustomerTests.TrackDisplayAdapter);
    }

    public override object[] query()
    {
        TrackDto[] dtoTracks = CatalogAdapter.Tracks();

        TrackDisplayAdapter[] adapters =
            new TrackDisplayAdapter[dtoTracks.Length];

        for(int index = 0; index < dtoTracks.Length; index++)
        {
            adapters[index] =
                new TrackDisplayAdapter(dtoTracks[index]);
        }

        return adapters;
    }
}
```

This class returns an array of objects. The query method takes no parameters, but must somehow return the track information associated with a recording. In this case, it makes a call to the *CatalogAdapter* (which retrieved the recording in the previous test) to get the tracks associated with the recording. The query method also converts the *TrackDto* objects into *TrackDisplayAdapter* objects just like the *CatalogAdapter* adapts the *RecordingDto*.

```
public class TrackDisplayAdapter
{
    private TrackDto dto;

    public TrackDisplayAdapter(TrackDto trackDto)
    {
        dto = trackDto;
    }

    public string Title()
    {
        return dto.title;
    }

    public string Duration()
    {
        return dto.duration.ToString();
    }

    public string GenreName()
    {
        return dto.genreName;
    }

    public string ArtistName()
    {
        return dto.artistName;
    }
}
```

When we run the tests, we get the following result:

CustomerTests.TrackDisplay			
Title()	**ArtistName()**	**GenreName()**	**Duration()**
Lonesome Day	Bruce Springsteen	Rock	4:08 expected
			248 actual
Into The Fire	Bruce Springsteen	Rock	5:04 expected
			304 actual

CustomerTests.TrackDisplay			
Title()	**ArtistName()**	**GenreName()**	**Duration()**
Waitin' On A Sunny Day	Bruce Springsteen	Rock	4:18 expected 258 actual
The Nothing Man	Bruce Springsteen	Rock	4:23 expected 263 actual
Let's Be Friends	Bruce Springsteen	Rock	4:21 expected 261 actual
The Fuse	Bruce Springsteen	Rock	5:37 expected 337 actual
Further On (Up The Road)	Bruce Springsteen	Rock	3:52 expected 232 actual
Mary's Place	Bruce Springsteen	Rock	6:03 expected 363 actual
The Rising	Bruce Springsteen	Rock	4:50 expected 290 actual
My City Of Ruins	Bruce Springsteen	Rock	5:00 expected 300 actual
Empty Sky	Bruce Springsteen	Rock	3:34 expected 214 actual
Worlds Apart	Bruce Springsteen	Rock	6:07 expected 367 actual
Paradise	Bruce Springsteen	Rock	5:39 expected 339 actual
You're Missing	Bruce Springsteen	Rock	5:11 expected 311 actual
Countin' On A Miracle	Bruce Springsteen	Rock	4:24 expected 284 actual

All the duration checks failed, which seems similar to the previous test (in which the check of the duration of the recording failed). Just as we did in the previous test, we make a note of it and we will return to it as soon as the script is fully automated.

Verifying Review Information

The review information is similar to the track information. In fact, we did create a new *RowFixture* called *ReviewDisplay* and an associated adapter named *ReviewDisplayAdapter*. (Their implementations are left as an exercise for the reader.) The problem the test exposes is related to the variability of the data. In the previous test, the Recording and Track information does not change, which is not the case with the review information—which is updated by reviewers all the time. Clearly, we do not want to write customer tests that need to be updated at random times. So what should we do? One option is to create a recording in the database as part of the script and subsequently remove it after the test is complete. Another option is to use a separate database that is a snapshot of the production database but not constantly modified by the users. The last option is to create a fake recording in the production database. This recording has well-known content and can't be changed by the users.

We choose to insert a well-known record in the database. It is the simplest alternative at the moment, and it allows us to use the actual deployment environment to run our tests. This solution is not immune from risk, however; someone can delete or change the fake recording in some way. And even though we believe the id will never be assigned, it is possible that someday it could overlap with a real recording, which would make our tests fail. There does not seem to be a perfect answer to this problem. If we choose a separate database, we have to employ some process to ensure that the schemas would stay synchronized, and so on. Given our solution, the script for verifying review information is as follows:

fit.ActionFixture		
start	CustomerTests.CatalogAdapter	
enter	FindByRecordingId	100001
check	Found	True
check	AverageRating	2

CustomerTests.ReviewDisplay		
ReviewerName()	Content()	Rating()
Sample Reviewer	Inspiration was low	1

CustomerTests.ReviewDisplay		
ReviewerName()	**Content()**	**Rating()**
Example Reviewer	Could be better	3
Test Reviewer	I thought it was great	4

When we run the tests for reviews, they all pass.

Invalid ID Script

The last part of the script that needs to be automated is the one that attempts to retrieve a recording that is not present in the database. Just as in the review script, the id chosen does not exist in the database and should never be assigned to a valid recording. If this assumption remains true, our test never has to change. The following is the test script:

fit.ActionFixture		
start	CustomerTests.CatalogAdapter	
enter	FindByRecordingId	100002
check	Found	False

This script does not require any changes to the *CatalogAdapter* because it uses existing methods. When we run the test, it passes as well.

Automation Summary

We began with a manual test script, and we ended up with a set of automated FIT scripts that are much less time-consuming to execute and less error-prone. In fact, they can be run every time the software is built. Also, they have identified a few problems. There seems to be an issue with durations on tracks as well as the overall duration on recording. There seems to be a mismatch in expectations between the programmers and the customer. In the next section, we will reconcile those differences.

Reconciling Viewpoints

The first thing to do is to verify that the test and the test data are correct. In this case, the customer verified that both are correct, so the problem is with the software. We need to fix the software to pass the customer tests. One thing that needs to be pointed out is the process that will be used to fix these problems.

Because we do not have a failing programmer test, it is clear that the programmers have misinterpreted the requirements in some way. To make sure that the programmer tests are in sync with the customer tests, we need to have at least one failing programmer test before we modify the code.

There are several reasons why we begin with a programmer test in such a case. First of all, the customer tests are usually too general to point to a specific problem spot in the code. Second, the failing customer test indicates a misunderstanding or a change in the user requirements, and we want to be able to use the programmer tests as a code-level requirement specification mechanism. So the programmer tests must be updated to reflect the change in the requirements. The failing customer tests that exist at this point are related to track and recording duration. We will address them one at a time.

Track Duration

Looking at the results, the track's duration is expected to be a string with the format "min:sec," and we get an integer value representing the duration in seconds. Doing a quick calculation, we see that the number is correct; it is just not formatted in the correct way. We need to convert from seconds to "min:sec" to meet the customer requirements. The simplest thing we can do to make the test pass is to modify the *Duration* method of *TrackDisplayAdapter*. After making this change, the customer tests pass, but we are left with the feeling that this conversion does not belong in the *TrackDisplayAdapter*. As stated previously, this class is supposed to be a very simple adapter with no logic present. Having added the application-specific logic to this class, we violated this requirement: this code cannot be present in the adapter. So let's find the right place.

To correctly follow our process, we first remove the conversion code from the adapter and run the customer tests. They now fail the same way they did before. We need to write a programmer test that exposes the problem revealed by the failing customer tests. The problem is on the server side when the *Track-Dto* is converted from the Track row. Let's write a programmer test in *Track-AssemblerFixture* to confirm this suspicion:

```
[Test]
public void Duration()
{
    Assert.AreEqual("1:40", trackDto.duration);
}
```

This test fails, and we think this is the right place to address this problem because the *RecordingAssembler* should be responsible for the conversion of the Track's duration. Let's add the conversion code to the *RecordingAssembler*'s

WriteTrack method. When we try to do that, we come across another problem: *TrackDto* has duration defined as int, not a string. This means that we need to make changes to the Recording.xsd schema file and regenerate the data transfer objects. When this process is complete, the *WriteTrack* method looks like this:

```
public static TrackDto WriteTrack(RecordingDataSet.Track track)
{
    TrackDto trackDto = new TrackDto();

    trackDto.id = track.Id;
    trackDto.title = track.Title;

    int minutes = track.Duration / 60;
    int seconds = track.Duration % 60;

    trackDto.duration = String.Format("{0}:{1}",
        minutes, seconds.ToString("00"));

    trackDto.genreName = track.Genre.Name;
    trackDto.artistName = track.Artist.Name;

    return trackDto;
}
```

We recompile and run all the programmer tests, and they succeed. In addition, we also run the customer tests. The ones associated with *TrackDuration* now pass. We weren't lucky enough with the Recording duration, so let's fix that now.

Recording Duration

The recording duration problem seems very similar to the problem with the Track's duration. So let's do the following:

■ Modify the *totalRunTime* test in the *RecordingAssemblerFixture* to expect "3:20" instead of "200".

■ Modify Recording.xsd schema file by changing the type of the *totalRunTime* from "int" to "string".

■ Add the formatting code to the *RecordingAssembler*.

After we made these changes, all the programmer tests pass, and all the customer tests pass. We did introduce a small code duplication related to formatting the duration strings in the *RecordingAssembler*. We'll leave removing it as an exercise for you.

Summary

In this chapter, we identified two different perspectives regarding completion: the customer and the programmer. These two perspectives need to be reconciled, but the customer's perspective determines whether the software is completed. The process of reconciliation is iterative and requires adding new programmer tests to expose the problem with the code as well as running customer tests frequently to confirm that the added programmer tests do fully expose the functional problem. Therefore, integrating customer tests into the development cycle becomes an important objective.

8

Driving Development with Customer Tests

In this chapter, we add the ability to add and delete a review from an existing recording. These capabilities are really two features, but due to the similarities in the implementation, we have grouped them together. Also, instead of implementing the functionality and then checking in with the customer to verify whether or not it's correct (as we did previously), we'll first work with the customer to define a set of customer tests and then implement the functionality to make the tests pass. This approach should eliminate the issues that we had implementing the previous feature when we, as the programmers, made some assumptions that turned out to be incorrect. Having customer tests prior to starting development is an ideal situation. Although we have not seen this situation very often, that does not make it any less desirable. In reality, you should push for the customer tests as soon as possible to alleviate the reconciliation of the differing viewpoints that we demonstrated in Chapter 7, "Customer Tests: Completing the First Feature." The longer you develop without customer tests, the greater the chance that the implementation will not match the customer's expectations.

The FIT Script

We need to write a test that verifies the correct behavior when adding a *Review* to a *Recording*. The script first verifies the existing state of the recording, then adds a review, and then deletes it. Here is the FIT script, "Add a review to an existing recording."

Add a review to an existing recording

This test, knowing the existing state, will add a review to a recording. After it's added, the test will retrieve the recording and verify that the review is correctly added. The last step is to remove the review from the recording, returning the database to its original state.

Before:

fit.ActionFixture		
start	*CustomerTests.CatalogAdapter*	
enter	*FindByRecordingId*	100001
check	*Found*	True
check	*AverageRating*	2

CustomerTests.ReviewDisplay		
ReviewerName()	**Content()**	**Rating()**
Sample Reviewer	Inspiration was low	1
Example Reviewer	Could be better	3
Test Reviewer	I thought it was great	4

Add the review:

fit.ActionFixture		
start	CustomerTests.ReviewAdapter	
enter	*FindByRecordingId*	100001
enter	*SetRating*	4
enter	*SetContent*	Test Content
enter	*SetReviewerName*	FIT Reviewer
enter	*AddReview*	
check	*ReviewAdded*	True
enter	*FindByRecordingId*	100001
check	*AverageRating*	3

Verify the contents of the review:

CustomerTests.ReviewDisplay		
ReviewerName()	**Content()**	**Rating()**
Sample Reviewer	Inspiration was low	1
Example Reviewer	Could be better	3
Test Reviewer	I thought it was great	4
FIT Reviewer	Test content	4

Remove the review:

To make sure that the test is repeatable, we need to remove the newly added review:

fit.ActionFixture		
enter	*DeleteReview*	Reviewer

To get this customer test to work, we need to create a new adapter that can add and delete a review. We call this class the *ReviewAdapter*, which is shown here:

```
public class ReviewAdapter : CatalogAdapter
{
    private string name;
    private string content;
    private int rating;
    private ReviewDto review;

    public bool ReviewAdded()
    {
        return (review != null);
    }

    public void DeleteReview(string reviewerName)
    {
    }

    public void AddReview(string nothing)
    {
    }

    public void SetReviewerName(string name)
    {
        this.name = name;
    }
```

```
public void SetRating(int rating)
{
   this.rating = rating;
}

public void SetContent(string content)
{
   this.content = content;
}
}
```

Instead of duplicating much of the *CatalogAdapter* code, we choose to have *AddReviewAdapter* inherit from *CatalogAdapter* to share the implementation. After the adapter compiles, it is time to run the script. Here are the failures. Add the review:

fit.ActionFixture		
start	*CustomerTests.AddReviewAdapter*	
enter	*FindByRecordingId*	100001
enter	*SetRating*	4
enter	*SetContent*	Test Content
enter	*SetReviewerName*	FIT Reviewer
enter	*AddReview*	
check	*ReviewAdded*	True expected
		False actual
enter	*FindByRecordingId*	100001
check	*AverageRating*	3 expected
		2 actual

Verify the contents of the review:

CustomerTests.ReviewDisplay		
ReviewerName()	**Content()**	**Rating()**
Sample Reviewer	Inspiration was low	1
Example Reviewer	Could be better	3
Test Reviewer	I thought it was great	4
FIT Reviewer missing	Test Content	4

We have three failures. Although we did expect this test to fail, the purpose of running the test was to give us an indication of whether or not the customer's expectations have been met. Obviously, there are many more tests needed to completely verify this functionality, but we use this one for the purposes of demonstration. Now let's go about the business of implementing the add and delete review functionality.

Implementing Add/Delete Review

Now that we have a customer test in place, we need to change the focus back to the actual implementation of the feature. To do this, we use programmer tests. After we have a failing customer test, we need to write a set of corresponding programmer tests that drive the development of the feature. But where should we start? We could start with the layer of our application closest to the failing customer tests—the service interface, or we could start with the layer closest to the database—data access.

Over the last few chapters, we have gradually built up the application architecture. Figure 8-1 demonstrates what our application structure looks like.

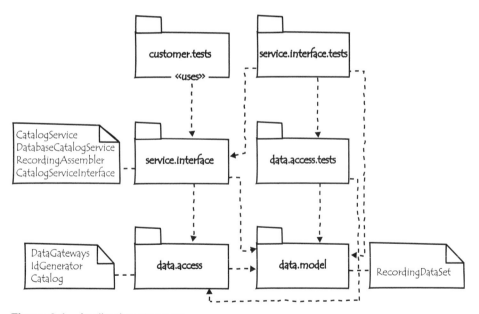

Figure 8-1   Application structure

The process of this architectural evolution was gradual and driven by the next small increment of the functionality that we needed to implement. Now we are attempting to add another increment of the functionality; however, the application's architecture appears to be sufficient to support the addition of this new functionality without making architectural changes—we simply can go to the appropriate points in the application and add the new functionality. We start with the data access layer to support the addition and deletion of reviews.

Let's define a test list for the add and delete review functionality:

Test List

- Add a review by an existing reviewer to a new recording, load the recording from the database, and verify that the added review is present.

- Add a review by a new reviewer to a new recording, load the recording from the database, and verify that the added review is present.

- Add a review by an existing reviewer to a new review, delete the added review, load the recording from the database, and verify that the added/deleted review is not present.

Given this test list, let's get to work on the implementation.

Changing the *Catalog* Class

We start with the *Catalog* class because it is the interface to our data access layer, and we need to make changes to this interface to support the additional functionality: *AddReview* and *DeleteReview*.

Our test list shows that we need to create a new recording for all the tests. We already have a test fixture that creates a new recording in the database—*RecordingFixture*—and we want to use it. Because the tests we are writing are all related to updating review information on a recording, we will create a new fixture for these new tests: *ReviewUpdateFixture*. This new fixture will extend the *RecordingFixture* to reuse its recording creation/deletion capabilities. Here are the tests:

```
using System;
using DataAccess;
using DataModel;
using NUnit.Framework;

[TestFixture]
public class ReviewUpdateFixture : RecordingFixture
{
    private static readonly string reviewerName = "ReviewUpdateFixture";

    private RecordingDataSet recordingDataSet = new RecordingDataSet();
    private RecordingDataSet.Recording loadedRecording;
```

```
[SetUp]
public new void SetUp()
{
   base.SetUp();

   RecordingDataSet loadedDataSet = new RecordingDataSet();
   loadedRecording = Catalog.FindByRecordingId(loadedDataSet,
      Recording.Id);
}


[TearDown]
public new void TearDown()
{
   base.TearDown();
}


[Test]
public void AddReviewWithExistingReviewer()
{
   int rating = 1;
   string content = "Review content";

   ReviewerGateway reviewerGateway =
      new ReviewerGateway(Connection);
   long reviewerId = reviewerGateway.Insert(recordingDataSet,
      reviewerName);
   RecordingDataSet.Reviewer reviewer =
      reviewerGateway.FindById(reviewerId, recordingDataSet);

   RecordingDataSet.Review review =
      Catalog.AddReview(recordingDataSet, reviewerName,
         content, rating, Recording.Id);
   Assert.IsNotNull(review);

   RecordingDataSet loadedFromDBDataSet = new RecordingDataSet();
   RecordingDataSet.Recording loadedFromDBRecording =
      Catalog.FindByRecordingId(loadedFromDBDataSet,
         Recording.Id);
   Assert.AreEqual(1, loadedFromDBRecording.GetReviews().Length);

   RecordingDataSet.Review loadedFromDBReview =
      loadedFromDBRecording.GetReviews()[0];

   ReviewGateway reviewGateway = new ReviewGateway(Connection);
   reviewGateway.Delete(loadedFromDBDataSet, loadedFromDBReview.Id);
   reviewerGateway.Delete(recordingDataSet, reviewerId);
}
```

```
[Test]
public void AddReviewWithoutExistingReviewer()
{
   int rating = 1;
   string content = "Review content";

   RecordingDataSet.Review review =
      Catalog.AddReview(recordingDataSet, reviewerName, content,
         rating, Recording.Id);
   Assert.IsNotNull(review);

   RecordingDataSet loadedFromDBDataSet = new RecordingDataSet();
   RecordingDataSet.Recording loadedFromDBRecording =
      Catalog.FindByRecordingId(loadedFromDBDataSet,
         Recording.Id);
   Assert.AreEqual(1, loadedFromDBRecording.GetReviews().Length);

   RecordingDataSet.Review loadedFromDBReview =
      loadedFromDBRecording.GetReviews()[0];

   ReviewGateway reviewGateway = new ReviewGateway(Connection);
   reviewGateway.Delete(loadedFromDBDataSet, loadedFromDBReview.Id);

   ReviewerGateway ReviewerGateway =
      new ReviewerGateway(Connection);
   long reviewerId = review.ReviewerId;
   ReviewerGateway.Delete(recordingDataSet, reviewerId);
}

[Test]
public void DeleteReview()
{
   int rating = 1;
   string content = "Review content";

   ReviewerGateway ReviewerGateway =
      new ReviewerGateway(Connection);
   long reviewerId = ReviewerGateway.Insert(recordingDataSet,
      reviewerName);
   RecordingDataSet.Reviewer reviewer =
      ReviewerGateway.FindById(reviewerId, recordingDataSet);

   RecordingDataSet.Review review =
      Catalog.AddReview(recordingDataSet, reviewerName,
         content, rating, Recording.Id);
   Catalog.DeleteReview(review.Id);

   RecordingDataSet loadedFromDB = new RecordingDataSet();
```

```
RecordingDataSet.Recording loadedFromDBRecording =
    Catalog.FindByRecordingId(loadedFromDB, Recording.Id);
Assert.AreEqual(0, loadedFromDBRecording.GetReviews().Length);
    }
}
```

In these tests, we verify two aspects of adding a review to a recording. One scenario is that the *Reviewer* has already been defined and we simply add the review. In this scenario, we need to know whether a reviewer with a given name already exists, and to support this we need to add a new method to the *ReviewerGateway*: *FindByName*.

In the other scenario, we have to also add the *Reviewer* to the database prior to adding the review. The test to delete a review adds the review and then verifies that it has been removed after the call to *DeleteReview*. When we try to compile this fixture, it fails because we have not added the *AddReview* and *DeleteReview* methods to the *Catalog* class. Let's do that now:

```
public static RecordingDataSet.Review AddReview(RecordingDataSet dataSet,
    string name, string content, int rating, long recordingId)
{
    SqlConnection connection = null;
    RecordingDataSet.Review review = null;

    try
    {
        connection = new SqlConnection(

            ConfigurationSettings.AppSettings.Get("Catalog.Connection"));
        connection.Open();

        RecordingDataSet.Recording recording =
            FindByRecordingId(dataSet, recordingId);

        ReviewerGateway reviewerGateway =
            new ReviewerGateway(connection);

        RecordingDataSet.Reviewer reviewer =
            reviewerGateway.FindByName(name, dataSet);

        if(reviewer == null)
        {
            long reviewerId = reviewerGateway.Insert(dataSet,name);
            reviewer = reviewerGateway.FindById(reviewerId,dataSet);
        }

        ReviewGateway reviewGateway = new ReviewGateway(connection);
        long reviewId = reviewGateway.Insert(dataSet, rating, content);
```

```
            review = reviewGateway.FindById(reviewId, dataSet);
            review.ReviewerId = reviewer.Id;
            review.Recording = recording;
            reviewGateway.Update(dataSet);
        }
        finally
        {
            if(connection != null)
                connection.Close();
        }

        return review;
    }

    public static void DeleteReview(long reviewId)
    {
        SqlConnection connection = null;

        try
        {
            connection = new SqlConnection(
                ConfigurationSettings.AppSettings.Get("Catalog.Connection"));
            connection.Open();

            RecordingDataSet recordingDataSet =
                new RecordingDataSet();

            ReviewGateway reviewGateway = new ReviewGateway(connection);
            reviewGateway.Delete(recordingDataSet, reviewId);
        }
        finally
        {
            if(connection != null)
                connection.Close();
        }

        return;
    }
```

This code compiles and runs successfully. Let's work on the *CatalogService*.

Changing the *CatalogService* Class

The next place we need to change is the *CatalogService* in the *ServiceInterface*. The current version of the *CatalogService* class is shown here:

```
using System;
using System.Collections;
using DataModel;
```

```
namespace ServiceInterface
{
    public abstract class CatalogService
    {
        public RecordingDto FindByRecordingId(long id)
        {
            RecordingDataSet.Recording recording = FindById(id);
            if(recording == null) return null;

            return RecordingAssembler.WriteDto(recording);
        }

        protected abstract
            RecordingDataSet.Recording FindById(long recordingId);
    }
}
```

We also have two subclasses of the *CatalogService* class: *DatabaseCatalog-Service* and *StubCatalogService*. *DatabaseCatalogService* implements the abstract *FindById* method by making a call to the database through the *Catalog* class; *StubCatalogService* works with an in-memory representation of a recording and does not make database calls. We used the stub implementation earlier as we were evolving the application architecture; the stub's purpose is to isolate the *ServiceInterface* code from the database. We have extracted most of the in-memory recording manipulation code that stub uses into another class—*InMemoryRecordingBuilder*—and this builder is used for testing *Recording-Assembler*.

At this point, we need to add new functionality to the *CatalogService* class; this, in turn, means that we will need to maintain two implementations of this functionality: *DatabaseCatalogService* and *StubCatalogService*. However, adding and deleting a review from the in-memory representation is not a worthy investment. What we really want to test is whether we can add or delete a review with a recording in the database. If we did this with the in-memory representation, we would also have to write the code that added and deleted the review from the *RecordingDataSet*. Let's leave the current class structure, but let's implement this new functionality only in the *DatabaseCatalogService* class. We will modify the code that we used in the *CatalogService* class and provide a default implementation for data access. Here are the changes:

```
using System;
using System.Collections;
using DataModel;

namespace ServiceInterface
```

```
{
    public abstract class CatalogService
    {
        public RecordingDto FindByRecordingId(long id)
        {
            RecordingDataSet.Recording recording = FindById(id);
            if(recording == null) return null;

            return RecordingAssembler.WriteDto(recording);
        }

        public ReviewDto AddReview(string reviewerName, string content,
            int rating, long recordingId)
        {
            RecordingDataSet.Review review =
                AddReviewToRecording(reviewerName,
                content, rating, recordingId);

            return RecordingAssembler.WriteReview(review);
        }

        public void DeleteReview(long reviewId)
        {
            DeleteReviewFromRecording(reviewId);
        }

        protected abstract
            RecordingDataSet.Recording FindById(long recordingId);

        protected virtual RecordingDataSet.Review AddReviewToRecording(
            string reviewerName, string content, int rating, long
                recordingId)
        {
            return null;
        }

        protected virtual void DeleteReviewFromRecording(long reviewId)
        {}
    }
}
```

The added code is in boldface. As you can see, instead of using an abstract method to defer the implementation of data access to the subclasses, the *CatalogService* class defines a pair of protected virtual methods (*AddReviewToRecording* and *DeleteReviewFromRecording*) with empty implementations. These default implementations of data access allow us to not modify the *StubCatalogService*. On the other hand, this version of the *CatalogService* seems somewhat awkward. We solve this problem in Chapter 11, "Service Layer Refactoring." Let's move on to implementing the *DatabaseCatalogService*.

Updating *DatabaseCatalogService*

We need to refine the test list for this step. Here is the list of the programmer tests that we need to implement:

- Add a review to a new recording and verify that the *ReviewDto* returned has the correct content.

- Add a review to a new recording, retrieve the recording by id from the service, and verify that the retrieved *RecordingDto* has the review just added.

- Add a review to a new recording, delete the review just added, retrieve the recording from the service, and verify that the retrieved recording does not have the deleted review.

Once again, these tests share similar *SetUp/TearDown* steps, and we can reuse the *RecordingFixture* to perform the required database access code. We choose to separate the tests for updating review information from the existing *DatabaseCatalogService* tests and place them into a new fixture: *DatabaseUpdateReviewFixture*. Here is the code for it:

```
[TestFixture]
public class DatabaseUpdateReviewFixture : RecordingFixture
{
    private static readonly string reviewerName =
      "DatabaseUpdateReviewFixture";
    private static readonly string reviewContent = "Fake Review Content";
    private static readonly int    rating = 3;

    private CatalogService service;

    [SetUp]
    public new void SetUp()
    {
        base.SetUp();
        service = new DatabaseCatalogService();
    }

    [TearDown]
    public new void TearDown()
    {
        base.TearDown();
    }
```

```
[Test]
public void AddReviewContent()
{
    ReviewDto dto = service.AddReview(reviewerName, reviewContent,
        rating, Recording.Id);

    Assert.AreEqual(reviewerName, dto.reviewerName);
    Assert.AreEqual(reviewContent, dto.reviewContent);
    Assert.AreEqual(rating, dto.rating);
}

[Test]
public void ReviewAddedToRecording()
{
    int beforeCount = Recording.GetReviews().Length;
    ReviewDto dto = service.AddReview(reviewerName,
        reviewContent, rating,
        Recording.Id);

    RecordingDto recordingDto =
        service.FindByRecordingId(Recording.Id);
    Assert.AreEqual(beforeCount+1, recordingDto.reviews.Length);
}

[Test]
public void ReviewDeletedFromRecording()
{
    int beforeCount = Recording.GetReviews().Length;

    ReviewDto dto = service.AddReview(reviewerName, reviewContent,
        rating, Recording.Id);

    service.DeleteReview(dto.id);

    RecordingDto recordingDto =
        service.FindByRecordingId(Recording.Id);
    Assert.AreEqual(beforeCount, recordingDto.reviews.Length);
}
}
```

These tests fail because we have not updated the *DatabaseCatalogService* class yet. Here are the two methods we have to add to the *DatabaseCatalog-Service* to make these tests pass:

```
protected override RecordingDataSet.Review AddReviewToRecording(
        string reviewerName, string content, int rating, long recordingId)
{
    RecordingDataSet dataSet = new RecordingDataSet();
```

```
    return Catalog.AddReview(dataSet, reviewerName, content,
      rating, recordingId);
}

protected override void DeleteReviewFromRecording(long reviewId)
{
    Catalog.DeleteReview(reviewId);
    return;
}
```

Now the tests pass, and we are ready to move on to the Web service.

Updating *CatalogServiceInterface*

This step is very similar to the step we just finished. Here is a test list:

■   Write the programmer tests for the *CatalogServiceInterface* (these will go into a new fixture called *UpdateCatalogGatewayFixture*).

■   Update the *CatalogServiceInterface* class by adding two new Web methods: *AddReview* and *DeleteReview*.

■   Hook up the Web methods to the *DatabaseCatalogService* class.

The new programmer tests verify the functionality when accessing the Web service. They are so similar to the tests for *DatabaseCatalogService* that we show only the one that has the most differences:

```
[Test]
public void ReviewDeletedFromRecording()
{
    ServiceGateway.RecordingDto recordingDto =
      gateway.FindByRecordingId(Recording.Id);
    Assert.IsNull(recordingDto.reviews);

    ServiceGateway.ReviewDto dto =
      gateway.AddReview(reviewerName, reviewContent, rating,
        Recording.Id);
    gateway.DeleteReview(dto.id);

    recordingDto = gateway.FindByRecordingId(Recording.Id);
    Assert.IsNull(recordingDto.reviews);
}
```

If you compare this test with the similar method in *DatabaseUpdate-ReviewFixture*, you see that the differences are in the serialization behavior: When we don't go through the Web service, we get back a *RecordingDto* with an empty collection of reviews; when we do go through the Web service layer, the resulting *RecordingDto* is *null* instead of an empty collection of reviews.

These Web service-specific serialization differences are the only new information these tests reveal. Because these tests do not reveal a lot more new information, and because there is a lot of overlap between these programmer tests and the customer tests, we felt that we were going to rely solely on the customer tests for verifying that the application works through the Web service. So we deleted the programmer tests that used the *CatalogGateway*.

Fixing *AddReviewAdapter*

Now that *CatalogServiceInterface* exposes the *AddReview* and *DeleteReview* services, we can modify the *AddReviewAdapter* in the customer tests to use the newly defined Web services.

```
public void AddReview(string nothing)
{
   review = Gateway.AddReview(name,
           content, rating, Recording.id);
}

public void DeleteReview(string nothing)
{
   if(review != null)
      Gateway.DeleteReview(review.id);
}
```

After we made the changes, we recompiled the customer tests and ran all the FIT scripts. All the customer and programmer tests pass, which is our indication that we are done implementing this feature.

Summary

In this chapter, we drove the development with customer tests. We began by first writing a customer test for the new feature. This test failed when it was run, as expected. We used this failing customer test as a very explicit form of requirements definition. However, the customer test is at too high a level to be able to drive development of the implementation. To drive the development, we turned back to programmer tests to flesh out the rest of the implementation. We started at the data access layer, drove the development back through the Web service, and eventually to the customer tests.

9

Driving Development with Customer Tests: Exposing a Failure Condition

In the previous chapter, we defined a customer test for adding and deleting a review from the database and then built the implementation accordingly. In this chapter, we enhance the *AddReview* Web service to prevent a reviewer from submitting multiple reviews for the same recording. When a reviewer attempts to do this, the Web service should not add the review to the database; it should return the id of the review that already exists in the database. Here is this requirement expressed as a customer test:

fit.ActionFixture		
start	*CustomerTests.ReviewAdapter*	
enter	*FindByRecordingId*	100001
enter	*SetRating*	4
enter	*SetContent*	Test Fit Content
enter	*SetReviewerName*	Example Reviewer
enter	*AddReview*	
check	*ReviewAdded*	False
check	*ExistingReviewId*	100002

To run this script, we need to add a method, named *ExistingReviewId*, to the *ReviewAdapter*. For now, let's fake the implementation and have the method always return 0. Let's run the script and see if we get the failures that we anticipate. Here is the output of the script:

fit.ActionFixture		
start	*CustomerTests.ReviewAdapter*	
enter	FindByRecordingId	100001
enter	SetRating	4
enter	SetContent	Test Fit Content
enter	SetReviewerName	Example Reviewer
enter	AddReview	
check	ReviewAdded	False expected
		True actual
check	ExistingReviewId	100002 expected
		0 actual

The script fails as anticipated because there is nothing in the implementation that prevents the user from adding a review to a recording as many times as he likes. In turn, we also run the programmer tests. Because all the programmer tests pass, there must be a missing programmer test. Let's write a programmer test that exposes the problem and drives the implementation.

Programmer Tests

The most appropriate place to write the first programmer test is in the *DataAccess* namespace. Because the test is similar to the other tests in *ReviewUpdateFixture*, we should put it in that test fixture. What should the test look like? Well, first it should insert a review into the database using the *Catalog.AddReview* function. After it is successfully added, the test should try to insert the review again. What should happen when this function is called the second time? *Catalog.AddReview* should throw an exception indicating that there is an existing review, and the exception object should contain the *id* of the existing review. Let's write a test that looks for an exception when the second review is added.

```
[Test]
public void AddTwoReviewsWithExistingReviewer()
{
    int rating = 1;
    string content = "Review content";
```

```
      ReviewerGateway reviewerGateway =
         new ReviewerGateway(Connection);
      long reviewerId =
         reviewerGateway.Insert(recordingDataSet, reviewerName);
      RecordingDataSet.Reviewer reviewer =
         reviewerGateway.FindById(reviewerId, recordingDataSet);

      RecordingDataSet.Review reviewOne =
         Catalog.AddReview(recordingDataSet, reviewerName,
         content, rating, Recording.Id);

      try
      {
         RecordingDataSet.Review reviewTwo =
            Catalog.AddReview(recordingDataSet,
            reviewerName, content, rating, Recording.Id);
         Assert.Fail("Expected an Exception");
      }
      catch(ExistingReviewException exception)
      {
         Assert.AreEqual(reviewOne.Id, exception.ExistingId);
      }
      finally
      {
         RecordingDataSet dbDataSet = new RecordingDataSet();
         RecordingDataSet.Recording dbRecording =
            Catalog.FindByRecordingId(dbDataSet,Recording.Id);
         RecordingDataSet.Review[] reviews =
                   dbRecording.GetReviews();

         ReviewGateway reviewGateway = new ReviewGateway(Connection);
         foreach(RecordingDataSet.Review existingReview in reviews)
         {
            reviewGateway.Delete(dbDataSet, existingReview.Id);
         }
         reviewerGateway.Delete(recordingDataSet, reviewerId);
      }
   }
```

We did not use NUnit's *ExpectedException* syntax here because we have test method-specific cleanup to do after the exception is thrown. We could have split this fixture in two and then used the *ExpectedException*, but it seems like more trouble than it is worth. When we compile the test, it fails because we have not defined the *ExistingReviewException* class. Let's do that now:

```
namespace DataAccess
{
   public class ExistingReviewException : ApplicationException
```

```
{
    private long id;

    public ExistingReviewException(long existingId)
    {
        id = existingId;
    }

    public long ExistingId
    {
        get
                { return id; }
    }
  }
}
```

The code now compiles. When we run the test, it fails because we have not changed the *Catalog.AddReview* function to throw the exception. Let's make that modification:

```
public static RecordingDataSet.Review AddReview(RecordingDataSet dataSet,
        string name, string content, int rating, long recordingId)
{
    SqlConnection connection = null;
    RecordingDataSet.Review review = null;

    try
    {
        connection = new SqlConnection(
          ConfigurationSettings.AppSettings.Get("Catalog.Connection"));
          connection.Open();

        RecordingDataSet.Recording recording =
            FindByRecordingId(dataSet, recordingId);

        ReviewerGateway reviewerGateway = new ReviewerGateway(connection);

        RecordingDataSet.Reviewer reviewer =
            reviewerGateway.FindByName(name, dataSet);

        if(reviewer == null)
        {
            long reviewerId = reviewerGateway.Insert(dataSet,name);
            reviewer = reviewerGateway.FindById(reviewerId,dataSet);
        }

        foreach(RecordingDataSet.Review existingReview in
                recording.GetReviews())
```

```
    {
      if(existingReview.Reviewer.Name.Equals(name))
         throw new ExistingReviewException(existingReview.Id);
    }

    ReviewGateway reviewGateway = new ReviewGateway(connection);
    long reviewId = reviewGateway.Insert(dataSet, rating, content);

    review = reviewGateway.FindById(reviewId, dataSet);
    review.ReviewerId = reviewer.Id;
    review.Recording = recording;
    reviewGateway.Update(dataSet);
  }
  finally
  {
    if(connection != null)
    connection.Close();
  }

  return review;
}
```

The boldface code shows the changes needed to throw an exception of type *ExistingReviewException* when there is an existing review by the same reviewer. Running the test indicates success. Now we need to run the customer tests as well and see what happens. When we run the customer test described at the beginning of the chapter, we get a *SoapException*, and the test does not pass. We need to make a change to the *ReviewAdapter* to make the test succeed. Here is the change:

```
public void AddReview(string nothing)
{
  try
  {
    review = Gateway.AddReview(name, content, rating,
                   Recording.id);
  }
  catch(SoapException exception)
  {
    review = null;
  }
}
```

This compiles; we first run the programmer tests, which all pass. Next we run the customer tests, and we get the result on the following page.

fit.ActionFixture		
start	*CustomerTests.ReviewAdapter*	
enter	*FindByRecordingId*	100001
enter	*SetRating*	4
enter	*SetContent*	Test Fit Content
enter	*SetReviewerName*	Example Reviewer
enter	*AddReview*	
check	*ReviewAdded*	False
check	*ExistingReviewId*	100002 expected 0 actual

We still have the implementation for *ExistingReviewId* in the *Review-Adapter* class, which returns 0. There is no way to implement this method as of yet because the *SoapException* does not explicitly contain the *ExistingId* field. How do we get the *SoapException* to contain the *ExistingId* information? Let's work on making this happen.

Propagating the Exception

There are a number of things we have to do to propagate the *ExistingReview-Exception* information to the client. We have to figure out how to augment the general Simple Object Access Protocol (SOAP) failure with the specific information needed when we try to add an additional review. One thing that jumps out immediately is that we do not want the client to be able to see the stack trace of our server code. This is a security issue because it gives people information about how our code is structured, and this could be exploited. So first, let's make sure that the clients cannot see the stack trace. This is accomplished by making a change to the Web.config file in the *ServiceInterface* directory. Here is the change:

```
<customErrors mode="RemoteOnly" />
```

After this change is made, the stack trace is no longer available to users who are not running on the local Web server.

Implementing a SOAP Fault

The next step is to propagate the *ExistingReviewException* information to the client using a SOAP fault. Previously, we were getting a *SoapException* without any detail. To make sure that we are getting the information we need, let's write a test that makes calls to the *CatalogGateway* that attempts to add the review twice, just as we did in the *Catalog*. Here is the test:

```
[TestFixture]
public class MultipleReviewFixture : RecordingFixture
{
   private static readonly string reviewerName =
      "DatabaseUpdateReviewFixture";
   private static readonly string reviewContent =
      "Fake Review Content";
   private static readonly int    rating = 3;

   private CatalogGateway gateway;
   private ServiceGateway.ReviewDto review;

   [Test]
   public void AddSecondReview()
   {
      gateway = new CatalogGateway();

      review = gateway.AddReview(reviewerName, reviewContent,
                  rating, Recording.Id);

      try
      {
         gateway.AddReview(reviewerName, reviewContent,
                 rating, Recording.Id);
         Assert.Fail("AddReview should have thrown an exception");
      }
      catch(SoapException exception)
      {
         Assert.AreEqual(
            SoapException.ClientFaultCode,
            exception.Code);
      }
      finally
      {
         ReviewGateway reviewGateway = new ReviewGateway(Connection);
         reviewGateway.Delete(RecordingDataSet, review.id);
      }
   }
}
```

MultipleReviewFixture inherits from *RecordingFixture*, which inserts a *Recording* into the database. The *AddSecondReview* test attempts to add the same review to the recording twice and verifies that it fails. At first, we are expecting it to return a *SoapException* with the *Code* property set to *Client-FaultCode*, which indicates that the reason the call did not succeed was due to a client-side error. When we compile and run this test, it fails because the *Code* property defaults to *ServerFaultCode*. Let's switch over to the server code and make this change. We need to modify the *AddReview* method in the *Service-Interface* to create the *SoapException* to be sent over the wire. Here is the first implementation:

```
[WebMethod]
public ReviewDto AddReview(string reviewerName, string content,
    int rating, long recordingId)
{
    ReviewDto review = null;

    try
    {
        review = service.AddReview(reviewerName, content,
            rating, recordingId);
    }
    catch(ExistingReviewException existingReview)
    {
        throw new SoapException(existingReview.Message,
            SoapException.ClientFaultCode);
    }

    return review;
}
```

After this is compiled and run, the test passes. All we have done, however, is to specify that a client problem has occurred. Let's move on and get more specific.

Turning back to the *MultipleReviewFixture*, we need to pass some additional information across the wire to indicate what is wrong. Because of the need for multiple tests with the same *SetUp*, we need to refactor the test code to eliminate the duplication. Here is the refactored test code that is equivalent to the previous code:

```
[TestFixture]
public class MultipleReviewFixture : RecordingFixture
{
    private static readonly string reviewerName =
        "DatabaseUpdateReviewFixture";
    private static readonly string reviewContent = "Fake Review Content";
    private static readonly int    rating = 3;

    private CatalogGateway gateway;
    private ServiceGateway.ReviewDto review;
    private SoapException soapException;

    [SetUp]
    public new void SetUp()
```

```
    {
        base.SetUp();

        gateway = new CatalogGateway();

        review = gateway.AddReview(reviewerName, reviewContent,
                rating, Recording.Id);

        try
        {
            gateway.AddReview(reviewerName, reviewContent,
                    rating, Recording.Id);
        }
        catch(SoapException exception)
        {
            soapException = exception;
        }
    }

    [TearDown]
    public new void TearDown()
    {
        ReviewGateway reviewGateway = new ReviewGateway(Connection);
        reviewGateway.Delete(RecordingDataSet, review.id);

        base.TearDown();
    }

    [Test]
    public void ExceptionThrown()
    {
        Assert.IsNotNull(soapException);
    }

    [Test]
    public void ClientFaultCode()
    {
        Assert.AreEqual(
            SoapException.ClientFaultCode,
            soapException.Code);
    }
}
```

When we compile and run this code, both tests pass, and we can move on to looking for the fault code. We need to use the *Detail* property of the *SoapException* to indicate why the call to *AddReview* failed. This is typically done using an XML document that contains the explicit fault code. The XML document is defined as follows:

```
<detail>
  <fault-code>ExistingReview</fault-code>
</detail>
```

We have decided that the detail fault code will be *ExistingReview* to indicate that a review by that reviewer already exists. Here is the test:

```
[Test]
public void DetailFaultCode()
{
    Assert.AreEqual("ExistingReview",
        XPathQuery(soapException.Detail, "//fault-code"));
}

private string XPathQuery(XmlNode node, string expression)
{
    XPathNavigator navigator = node.CreateNavigator();

    string selectExpr = expression;
    navigator.MoveToRoot();
    XPathExpression expr = navigator.Compile(selectExpr);

    XPathNodeIterator index = navigator.Select(expr);
    index.MoveNext();
    return index.Current.Value.Trim();
}
```

When we run this test, it fails because there is no detail being added to the *SoapException*. Let's move over to the server and make it work. We need to make the following highlighted changes to the *AddReview* method to make this test pass:

```
[WebMethod]
public ReviewDto AddReview(string reviewerName, string content,
        int rating, long recordingId)
{
    ReviewDto review = null;

    try
    {
        review = service.AddReview(reviewerName, content,
                rating, recordingId);
    }
    catch(ExistingReviewException existingReview)
    {
```

```
        XmlDocument document = new XmlDocument();
        XmlElement detail = document.CreateElement("detail");
        document.AppendChild(detail);

        XmlElement code = document.CreateElement("fault-code");
        detail.AppendChild(code);
        XmlText faultCode =
                    document.CreateTextNode("ExistingReview");
        code.AppendChild(faultCode);

        throw new SoapException(existingReview.Message,
            SoapException.ClientFaultCode,
            Context.Request.Url.ToString(),
            document.DocumentElement);

    }

    return review;
}
```

When this code compiles, the tests pass. Let's continue on. The next step is to pass the *id* of the existing review to the client. We will be modifying the XML document to include this information as well. The new XML document is defined as follows:

```
<detail>
    <fault-code>ExistingReview</fault-code>
    <existing-id>1001</existing-id>
</detail>
```

Given this new requirement, let's add a test to look for the *existing-id* field:

```
[Test]
public void ExistingReviewId()
{
    Assert.AreEqual(review.id,
        Int64.Parse(XPathQuery(soapException.Detail,
                "//existing-id")));
}
```

Using the standard practice of compiling and running the tests, this test does not pass. We need to fix the implementation on the server and add the *existing-id* field to the XML document. Here is the updated *AddReview* method with the changes highlighted:

```
[WebMethod]
public ReviewDto AddReview(string reviewerName, string content,
```

```
               int rating, long recordingId)
    {
        ReviewDto review = null;

        try
        {
            review = service.AddReview(reviewerName, content,
                    rating, recordingId);
        }
        catch(ExistingReviewException existingReview)
        {
            XmlDocument document = new XmlDocument();
            XmlElement detail = document.CreateElement("detail");
            document.AppendChild(detail);

            XmlElement code = document.CreateElement("fault-code");
            detail.AppendChild(code);
            XmlText faultCode =
                        document.CreateTextNode("ExistingReview");
            code.AppendChild(faultCode);

            XmlElement existingId =
                        document.CreateElement("existing-id");
            detail.AppendChild(existingId);
            XmlText id =
                    document.CreateTextNode(
                        existingReview.ExistingId.ToString());
            existingId.AppendChild(id);

            throw new SoapException(existingReview.Message,
                SoapException.ClientFaultCode,
                Context.Request.Url.ToString(),
                document.DocumentElement);

        }

        return review;
    }
```

After this code is compiled, all the programmer tests pass as expected. When we run the customer tests, we are still left with a single failing customer test. Because we did the work to send the data to the client, we can implement the *ReviewAdapter.ExistingReviewId* method. Here is the updated *ReviewAdapter*:

```
public class ReviewAdapter : CatalogAdapter
{
    private string name;
    private string content;
```

```
private int     rating;
private ReviewDto review;
private long existingReviewId;

public void AddReview(string nothing)
{
   try
   {
      review = Gateway.AddReview(name, content, rating,
               Recording.id);
   }
   catch(SoapException soapException)
   {
      review = null;
      existingReviewId = Int64.Parse(
         XPathQuery(soapException.Detail,
                         "//existing-id"));
   }
}

public void DeleteReview(string reviewerName)
{
   Gateway.DeleteReview(review.id);
}

public long ExistingReviewId()
{ return existingReviewId; }

public bool ReviewAdded()
{ return (review != null); }

public void SetReviewerName(string name)
{ this.name = name; }

public void SetRating(int rating)
{ this.rating = rating; }

public void SetContent(string content)
{ this.content = content; }

private string XPathQuery(XmlNode node, string expression)
{
   XPathNavigator navigator = node.CreateNavigator();

   string selectExpr = expression;
   navigator.MoveToRoot();
   XPathExpression expr = navigator.Compile(selectExpr);
```

```
        XPathNodeIterator index =
            navigator.Select(expr);

        index.MoveNext();

        return index.Current.Value.Trim();
    }
}
```

When we compile and run all the tests (customer and programmer), they pass. We are done with implementing the functionality. However, there is some cleanup we need to do before we can move on. In the previous chapter, we made an argument that the customer tests are the best way to test the system through the Web service. In this chapter, we again wrote programmer tests that used the *CatalogGateway* when we were implementing the functionality. The tests in *MultipleReviewFixture* verified the failure condition and that the server built a *SoapException* with the detail information related to the failure. However, the scope of these tests is too large. They require the entire system to run and are really duplicates of the customer tests, so we will remove the *Multiple-ReviewFixture*. If we remove the *MultipleReviewFixture*, we will lose the test coverage related to mapping an *ExistingReviewException* into a *SoapException*. We can test this mapping without having to transport it across the Web service, however. Let's do that now.

There is code in the *CatalogServiceInterface.AddReview* method that builds the *SoapException* with the information related to the *ExistingReviewerException*. We can separate this code into a new class called *ExistingReview-Mapper*, which maps the information from an *ExistingReviewException* into a *SoapException* with the proper detail filled in. Let's write the *ExistingReview-MapperFixture*:

```
[TestFixture]
public class ExistingReviewMapperFixture
{
    private static readonly long id = 12;
    private SoapException soapException;

    [SetUp]
    public void SetUp()
    {
        ExistingReviewException exception = new
                ExistingReviewException(id);
        soapException = ExistingReviewMapper.Map(exception);
    }
```

```
    [Test]
    public void ClientFaultCode()
    {
       Assert.AreEqual(SoapException.ClientFaultCode,
          soapException.Code);
    }

    [Test]
    public void FaultCode()
    {
       string faultCode = XPathQuery(soapException.Detail,
                "//fault-code");
       Assert.AreEqual(ExistingReviewMapper.existingReviewFault,
                         faultCode);
    }

    [Test]
    public void ExistingIdField()
    {
       string existingId = XPathQuery(soapException.Detail,
                "//existing-id");
       Assert.AreEqual(id, Int64.Parse(existingId));
    }

    private static string XPathQuery(XmlNode node, string expression)
    {
       // same code as shown in previous sections
    }
}
```

The resulting implementation of *ExistingReviewMapper* looks like this:

```
namespace ServiceInterface
{
   public class ExistingReviewMapper
   {
      private static readonly string operation = "AddReview";

      public static readonly string rootElement = "detail";
      public static readonly string faultCodeElement = "fault-code";
      public static readonly string existingIdElement = "existing-id";
      public static readonly string invalidFieldElement =
               "invalid-field";
      public static readonly string existingReviewFault =
               "ExistingReview";

      private static XmlDocument Make(string faultCode,
         string fieldName, string fieldValue)
```

```
        {
            XmlDocument document = new XmlDocument();
            XmlElement detail = document.CreateElement(rootElement);
            document.AppendChild(detail);

            XmlElement code = document.CreateElement(faultCodeElement);
            detail.AppendChild(code);
            XmlText codeNode =
                        document.CreateTextNode(faultCode.ToString());
            code.AppendChild(codeNode);

            XmlElement field = document.CreateElement(fieldName);
            detail.AppendChild(field);
            XmlText fieldNode = document.CreateTextNode(fieldValue);
            field.AppendChild(fieldNode);

            return document;
        }

        public static SoapException Map(ExistingReviewException exception)
        {
            XmlDocument document =
                Make(existingReviewFault, existingIdElement,
                exception.ExistingId.ToString());

            return new SoapException(exception.Message,
                SoapException.ClientFaultCode,
                operation, document.DocumentElement);
        }
    }
}
```

The code compiles, and the tests pass. Let's replace the code in the *Catalog-ServiceInterface.AddReview* method to use the *ExistingReviewMapper* class:

```
[WebMethod]
public ReviewDto AddReview(string reviewerName, string content,
    int rating, long recordingId)
{
    ReviewDto review = null;

    try
    {
        review = service.AddReview(reviewerName, content,
            rating, recordingId);
    }
    catch(ExistingReviewException existingReview)
    {
```

```
            throw ExistingReviewMapper.Map(existingReview);
    }

    return review;
}
```

We compile and run the programmer tests, and they all pass. We also run the customer tests, and they pass as well. By separating the functionality that maps the *ExistingReviewException* into a *SoapException* out, we can now use programmer tests to determine whether the mapping is correct and customer tests to verify that the system works end-to-end as expected.

Summary

In this chapter, we started with a customer test and wrote programmer tests to drive the implementation. This eliminated the need for checking with the customer to determine the correctness of the application. After the test passed, we were finished. The scope of the customer/programmer tests, as demonstrated in the chapter, is very different. The customer test verifies that the system works as the customer expects (this working system includes the database and the Web service infrastructure). On the other hand, the programmer tests try to isolate themselves as much as possible and focus on what the application does independently of the infrastructure.

In the next chapter, we finally solve a problem that has plagued us over the last two chapters. When we built the Data Access code in Chapter 5, there were few if any errors that could occur. However, we ran into a few more issues as we started updating the database. In the next chapter, we use transaction support from the database to ensure that each test runs in the same environment as the previous test.

10

Programmer Tests: Using Transactions

In this chapter, we use database transaction support to write programmer tests that are easier to read and are much better at ensuring that the database is left in the correct state when a test is completed. Having to restore the database to its previous state leads to test code such as *AddTwoReviewsWithExisting-Reviewer,* which we wrote in the previous chapter. This test has a lot of code that cleans up after itself. In fact, it is hard to see what the test is and what the cleanup code is.

The test code was relatively straightforward in Chapter 5, "Programmer Tests: Using TDD with ADO.NET," when we were doing read-only access to the database. However, as we added update capability with the possibility of failure we had to write a lot more cleanup code. It is time to address this problem with a different technique. As we mentioned in Chapter 5, it is possible to use the transactional rollback functionality in the database to automatically remove the data created by the programmer tests. This seems like a cleaner approach in light of the update requirements.

> **Note** If you are not familiar with transactions in ADO.NET, see Appendix B, "Transactions in ADO.NET," for a brief overview or see *Pragmatic ADO.NET* by Shawn Wildermuth.

Programmer Tests

Let's outline the approach we want to take with the integration of transactions into the programmer tests. The existing tests for database access follow a similar pattern:

- *SetUp* creates the persistent data in the database

- *Test* manipulates the persistent data

- *TearDown* restores the database to the initial state

However, there are several tests that are not as simple. This is due in part to the need to delete the data that is inserted into the database as part of the test. Here is an example from the *ReviewUpdateFixture*:

```
[Test]
public void AddTwoReviewsWithExistingReviewer()
{
    int rating = 1;
    string content = "Review content";

    ReviewerGateway reviewerGateway =
        new ReviewerGateway(Connection);
    long reviewerId =
        reviewerGateway.Insert(recordingDataSet, reviewerName);
    RecordingDataSet.Reviewer reviewer =
        reviewerGateway.FindById(reviewerId, recordingDataSet);

    RecordingDataSet.Review reviewOne =
        Catalog.AddReview(recordingDataSet, reviewerName,
        content, rating, Recording.Id);

    try
    {
        RecordingDataSet.Review reviewTwo =
            Catalog.AddReview(recordingDataSet,
            reviewerName, content, rating, Recording.Id);
        Assert.Fail("Expected an Exception");
    }
    catch(ExistingReviewException exception)
    {
        Assert.AreEqual(reviewOne.Id, exception.ExistingId);
    }
    finally
    {
        RecordingDataSet dbDataSet = new RecordingDataSet();
        RecordingDataSet.Recording dbRecording =
            Catalog.FindByRecordingId(dbDataSet,Recording.Id);
```

```
        RecordingDataSet.Review[] reviews =
dbRecording.GetReviews();

        ReviewGateway reviewGateway = new ReviewGateway(Connection);
        foreach(RecordingDataSet.Review existingReview in reviews)
        {
            reviewGateway.Delete(dbDataSet, existingReview.Id);
        }
        reviewerGateway.Delete(recordingDataSet, reviewerId);
    }
}
```

As you can see, the cleanup code is placed in the *finally* block of the test instead of the *TearDown* method. This is typical for tests that make slight adjustments to the test data. We cannot rely on the *TearDown* method to explicitly remove the slightly modified test data.

We could get creative with overriding *SetUp/TearDown* methods in the test classes that share common test data but require slight customizations to it, but this approach is error-prone because if we forget to call the base class' *TearDown* method, we will leave the persistent garbage in the database. We also could create separate fixtures for each test that requires a customized *SetUp/TearDown* method. Both of these approaches are somewhat similar, and in the end all require us to implement code to reset the database back to its initial state. Because we want a solution that lets us focus on what we are testing as opposed to worrying about writing code that resets the database, let's try a different approach.

Transaction Manager

The first part of the solution is to create a class named *TransactionManager*. This class will be responsible for the following:

- Begin a transaction; we do not intend to support nested transactions, and any attempt to start a second transaction associated with the thread of the caller while there is an existing transaction in progress should fail.

- Roll back the transaction.

- Commit the transaction.

- Retrieve the current transaction.

- Maintain an association between the calling thread and the transaction.

We did implement the *TransactionManager* one programmer test at a time, but for the sake of brevity, the following is the complete list of programmer tests for the *TransactionManager*:

```
[TestFixture]
public class TransactionManagerFixture : ConnectionFixture
{
    private SqlTransaction transaction;

    [SetUp]
    public void BeginTransaction()
    {
        transaction = TransactionManager.Begin(Connection);
    }

    [TearDown]
    public void CommitTransaction()
    {
        if(TransactionManager.Transaction() != null)
        {
            TransactionManager.Commit();
        }
    }

    [Test]
    public void BeginNewTransaction()
    {
        Assert.IsNotNull(transaction);
    }

    [Test]
    public void GetCurrentTransaction()
    {
        Assert.AreSame(transaction,
            TransactionManager.Transaction());
    }

    [Test]
    public void GetCurrentTransactionNoTransactionInProgress()
    {
        TransactionManager.Commit();
        Assert.IsNull(TransactionManager.Transaction());
    }

    [Test]
    public void Commit()
    {
        TransactionManager.Commit();
        Assert.IsNull(TransactionManager.Transaction());
    }

    [Test]
    public void Rollback()
```

```
    {
       TransactionManager.Rollback();
       Assert.IsNull(TransactionManager.Transaction());
    }

    [Test, ExpectedException(typeof(ApplicationException))]
    public void CommitNullTransaction()
    {
       TransactionManager.Commit();
       TransactionManager.Commit();
    }

    [Test,ExpectedException(typeof(ApplicationException))]
    public void BeginNewTransactionTwice()
    {
       TransactionManager.Begin(Connection);
    }
  }
```

The corresponding implementation of the *TransactionManager* is shown here:

```
using System;
using System.Data.SqlClient;
using System.Collections;
using System.Threading;

namespace DataAccess
{
   public class TransactionManager
   {
     private static Hashtable transactions = new Hashtable();

     public static SqlTransaction Begin(SqlConnection connection)
     {
       SqlTransaction transaction = Transaction();

       if(transaction == null)
       {
          transaction = connection.BeginTransaction();
          transactions[Thread.CurrentThread] = transaction;
       }
       else
       {
          throw new
             ApplicationException("Transaction in progress");
       }

       return transaction;
     }
```

```
public static SqlTransaction Transaction()
{
   Thread currentThread = Thread.CurrentThread;
   SqlTransaction transaction =
      (SqlTransaction)transactions[currentThread];
   return transaction;
}

public static void Commit()
{
   SqlTransaction transaction = Transaction();

   if(transaction == null)
   {
      throw new
      ApplicationException("No transaction in progress");
   }

   transaction.Commit();
   End();
}

public static void Rollback()
{
   SqlTransaction transaction = Transaction();

   if(transaction == null)
   {
      throw new
      ApplicationException("No transaction in progress");
   }

   transaction.Rollback();
   End();
}

private static void End()
{
   transactions.Remove(Thread.CurrentThread);
}
   }
}
```

The *TransactionManager* uses a *Hashtable* to maintain the one-to-one mapping between the calling thread and its associated transaction. The rest of the functionality is done by the *SqlTransaction* class.

Integrating *TransactionManager* with the Tests and Application Code

The execution of each test using transactions follows the same pattern:

- The *SetUp* method starts a new transaction and inserts the required persistent entities into the database.

- It runs the test.

- The *TearDown* method rolls back the transaction.

Instead of writing this over and over, we will capture this pattern in a class named *DatabaseFixture* that will allow us to consistently enforce the pattern:

```
[TestFixture]
public abstract class DatabaseFixture : ConnectionFixture
{
   [SetUp]
   public void StartTransaction()
   {
      TransactionManager.Begin(Connection);
      Insert();
   }

   public abstract void Insert();

   [TearDown]
   public void Rollback()
   {
      TransactionManager.Rollback();
   }
}
```

> **Note**   We defined an abstract method named *Insert* for derived classes to insert entities into the database that are needed by the test fixture. We do not need the corresponding *Delete* functionality in the *TearDown* method because we are using the rollback mechanism that is provided by the database.

Here is a version of the *ArtistFixture* class modified to work with the newly created *DatabaseFixture*:

```
[TestFixture]
public class ArtistFixture : DatabaseFixture
{
   private static readonly string artistName = "Artist";
```

```
private ArtistGateway gateway;
private RecordingDataSet recordingDataSet;
private long artistId;

public override void Insert()
{
   recordingDataSet = new RecordingDataSet();
   gateway = new ArtistGateway(Connection);

   artistId = gateway.Insert(recordingDataSet,artistName);
}

[Test]
public void RetrieveArtistFromDatabase()
{
   RecordingDataSet loadedFromDB = new RecordingDataSet();
   RecordingDataSet.Artist loadedArtist =
      gateway.FindById(artistId, loadedFromDB);

   Assert.AreEqual(artistId,loadedArtist.Id);
   Assert.AreEqual(artistName, loadedArtist.Name);
}

[Test]
public void DeleteArtistFromDatabase()
{
   RecordingDataSet emptyDataSet = new RecordingDataSet();
   long deletedArtistId =
      gateway.Insert(emptyDataSet,"Deleted Artist");
   gateway.Delete(emptyDataSet,deletedArtistId);

   RecordingDataSet.Artist deletedArtist =
      gateway.FindById(deletedArtistId, emptyDataSet);
   Assert.IsNull(deletedArtist);
}

[Test]
public void UpdateArtistInDatabase()
{
   RecordingDataSet.Artist artist = recordingDataSet.Artists[0];
   artist.Name = "Modified Name";
   gateway.Update(recordingDataSet);

   RecordingDataSet updatedDataSet = new RecordingDataSet();
   RecordingDataSet.Artist updatedArtist = gateway.FindById(artistId,
      updatedDataSet);
   Assert.AreEqual("Modified Name", updatedArtist.Name);
}
}
```

If you compare this code to the previous version of the *ArtistFixture* class (see Chapter 5), you will notice the following differences:

■ The *ArtistFixture* inherits from *DatabaseFixture* instead of *Connection-Fixture* to be able to use the transaction capability.

■ Instead of using the *[SetUp]* attribute to indicate which method is to be called prior to test execution, we implement the *Insert* method to insert test-specific data into the database.

■ There is no *TearDown* method because it is handled by the *Database-Fixture*, which calls *Rollback* on the transaction to reset the database.

■ All the test methods no longer delete persistent entities from the database.

When we compile and run these tests, they fail because we need to make a small change in the constructor of the *ArtistGateway* class, which is in bold-face in the following code:

```
public ArtistGateway(SqlConnection connection)
{
   this.connection = connection;

   command = new SqlCommand(
      "select id, name from artist where id = @id",
      connection);
   command.Parameters.Add("@id",SqlDbType.BigInt);
   command.Transaction = TransactionManager.Transaction();

   adapter = new SqlDataAdapter(command);
   builder = new SqlCommandBuilder(adapter);
}
```

We needed to associate the SQL command with the current transaction. When this code is compiled and run, the tests fail because we need to make a similar change to the *IdGenerator* class. After updating *IdGenerator*, we compile and run the tests again, and this time they all pass. To complete this part of the implementation, we need to make the same changes to the following classes:

■ *LabelFixture* and *LabelGateway*

■ *GenreFixture and GenreGateway*

■ *ReviewFixture* and *ReviewGateway*

■ *ReviewerFixture* and *ReviewerGateway*

■ *TrackFixture* and *TrackGateway*

We completed these one at a time, each time verifying that the tests pass. It is time for us to tackle the *RecordingGatewayFixture* and *RecordingGateway* classes. The changes here are different because the *RecordingGatewayFixture* (and other test fixtures, for that matter) inherit from a class named *Recording-Fixture*, whose responsibility is to insert a recording into the database. We need to modify the *RecordingFixture* to inherit from *DatabaseFixture* to take advantage of the transactional capability. However, it is not as simple as just doing that. The test fixtures that inherited from *RecordingFixture* also customized the recording after it was inserted into the database. This means that we have to put in a method that the *RecordingFixture* calls to customize the *Recording* after it has inserted the *Recording* entity into the database. Figure 10-1 describes the structure of the test fixtures and their respective responsibilities after implementing these changes.

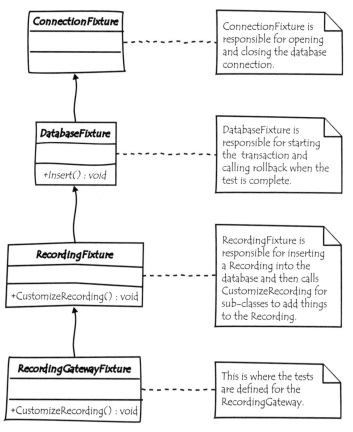

Figure 10-1   Test fixture hierarchy

The code changes for *RecordingFixture* are highlighted in this code:

```
[TestFixture]
public abstract class RecordingFixture : DatabaseFixture
{
    private RecordingBuilder builder = new RecordingBuilder();
    private RecordingDataSet dataSet;
    private RecordingDataSet.Recording recording;

    public override void Insert()
    {
        dataSet = builder.Make(Connection);
        recording = dataSet.Recordings[0];
        CustomizeRecording();
    }

    public virtual void CustomizeRecording()
    {}

    public RecordingBuilder Builder
    {
        get { return builder; }
    }

    public RecordingDataSet.Recording Recording
    {
        get { return recording; }
    }

    public RecordingDataSet RecordingDataSet
    {
        get { return dataSet; }
    }
}
```

We also had to change the *RecordingGatewayFixture* due to the changes in the *RecordingFixture*. The tests remained the same, so only the changes are shown in the following code:

```
[TestFixture]
public class RecordingGatewayFixture : RecordingFixture
{
    private RecordingGateway gateway;

    public override void CustomizeRecording()
    {
        gateway = Builder.RecordingGateway;
    }
```

```
// Tests were the same as shown previously
}
```

Finally, when we run these tests, they all fail because we did not modify the *RecordingGateway* to use transactions. The change we need to make to the constructor of *RecordingGateway* is highlighted as follows:

```
public RecordingGateway(SqlConnection connection)
{
    this.connection = connection;

    command = new SqlCommand(
      "select id, title, releaseDate, artistId, labelId" +
      "from recording where id = @id", connection);
    command.Parameters.Add("@id",SqlDbType.BigInt);
    command.Transaction = TransactionManager.Transaction();

    adapter = new SqlDataAdapter(command);
    builder = new SqlCommandBuilder(adapter);
}
```

Now when we run the *RecordingGatewayFixture* tests, they all pass. We then updated the following test fixtures that also inherit from *RecordingFixture*:

- *RecordingArtistFixture*

- *RecordingLabelFixture*

- *RecordingReviewsFixture*

- *ReviewRecordingFixture*

- *TrackRecordingFixture*

- *DatabaseCatalogServiceFixture*

- *DatabaseUpdateReviewFixture*

- *ReviewUpdateFixture*

The changes were similar to the ones that we made for the *Recording-GatewayFixture*. When we ran the tests, they all passed except four tests in *ReviewUpdateFixture*. In looking at the code, we see the big difference is that this code makes calls to the *Catalog* class, which also needs to be modified to know about transactions. Instead of having the four failing tests every time we run NUnit, we mark the *ReviewUpdateFixture* with the *[Ignore]* attribute. After we fix the *Catalog* class, we will remove the attribute and see whether we have corrected the problem.

Programmer Tests: *Catalog* Class

In the previous section, we made the gateways transaction-capable, and the transaction boundary was controlled by the test fixtures. The *Catalog* class has a dual purpose. On one hand, interface methods of the *Catalog* class need to manage the transactional boundaries of the application when that class is used by the rest of the application. On the other hand, the *Catalog* class interface methods need to participate in the transactions managed by programmer tests when the class is being tested. This behavior is similar to what would be achieved by using the transactional serviced components in COM+ that have a *Required* transaction attribute.

During the execution of the application, the COM+ Enterprise Services run time would intercept all the interface calls to the serviced components, check their transactional attribute, and begin the new transaction on the component's behalf if there is no transaction in progress. Because we are not using the automatic transaction management provided by Enterprise Services (for various reasons), we have to develop a similar mechanism for the application.

Let's start with the *CatalogFixture* class. This class needs to inherit from *DatabaseFixture* instead of *ConnectionFixture*, rename the *SetUp* method to *Insert*, and remove the *TearDown* method. The changes are highlighted here:

```
[TestFixture]
public class CatalogFixture : DatabaseFixture
{
    // member variables are the same

    public override void Insert()
    {
        // same as previous
    }

    // tests are the same
}
```

When we compile and run these tests, they all fail with the same error we got when we ran the *ReviewUpdateFixture*. We have to make the *Catalog* class transaction-enabled to fix these failures. We will begin with the *FindBy-RecordingId* method. Here is the existing version of this method:

```
public static RecordingDataSet.Recording FindByRecordingId(
        RecordingDataSet recordingDataSet, long recordingId)
{
    SqlConnection connection = null;
    RecordingDataSet.Recording recording = null;
```

```
try
{
    connection = new SqlConnection(
      ConfigurationSettings.AppSettings.Get("Catalog.Connection"));
      connection.Open();

    RecordingGateway recordingGateway =
          new RecordingGateway(connection);
    recording = recordingGateway.FindById(recordingId,
          recordingDataSet);
    if(recording != null)
    {
      long artistId = recording.ArtistId;
      ArtistGateway artistGateway = new ArtistGateway(connection);
      RecordingDataSet.Artist artist =
        artistGateway.FindById(artistId, recordingDataSet);

      long labelId = recording.LabelId;
      LabelGateway labelGateway = new LabelGateway(connection);
      RecordingDataSet.Label label =
        labelGateway.FindById(labelId, recordingDataSet);

      GenreGateway genreGateway = new GenreGateway(connection);
      TrackGateway trackGateway = new TrackGateway(connection);
      foreach(RecordingDataSet.Track track in
      trackGateway.FindByRecordingId(recordingId,
      recordingDataSet))
      {
        artistId = track.ArtistId;
        long genreId = track.GenreId;
        artist = artistGateway.FindById(artistId,
          recordingDataSet);
        RecordingDataSet.Genre genre =
          genreGateway.FindById(genreId, recordingDataSet);
      }

      ReviewGateway reviewGateway = new ReviewGateway(connection);
      ReviewerGateway reviewerGateway = new
        ReviewerGateway(connection);
      foreach(RecordingDataSet.Review review in

        reviewGateway.FindByRecordingId(recordingId,
          recordingDataSet))
      {
        long reviewerId = review.ReviewerId;

        RecordingDataSet.Reviewer reviewer =
          reviewerGateway.FindById(reviewerId,
```

```
                    recordingDataSet);
            }
        }
    }
    finally
    {
        if(connection != null)
            connection.Close();
    }

    return recording;
}
```

Here is some pseudo-code that describes how we want the method to behave:

```
if(transaction is in progress)
{
    execute application code
}
else
{
    connect to the database
    start a transaction
    execute application code
    if(successful)
        commit the transaction
    else
        rollback the transaction

    close the connection to the database
}
```

This pseudo-code indicates a pretty large change to the existing code, and we will have to repeat it for every single method of the *Catalog* class! (Also note that the application logic code block will have to be called from two places, too. This looks pretty nasty!) Instead of blindly doing this, let's look for a more general solution.

Refactoring the *Catalog* class

What we need is a mechanism to handle transactional aspects of the method invocation separately from the execution of the application code.

There are several approaches we could do to achieve this. For example, we could rely on code generation to create an implementation class, say *CatalogSkeleton*, which would inherit from the *Catalog* class and would override all the methods to include the transaction management code. We want to make the methods on the *Catalog* class nonstatic and virtual to support this option. We could write a proxy class, say *CatalogProxy*, which would have the same methods as the *Catalog* class, and would use reflection-based method delegation and add transaction management code. All these approaches sound overly complicated, and one of the consequences of complexity is that they would be equally hard to understand. Let's look for a more explicit solution that will also give us some flexibility in testing. Let's focus first on the code that manages the transaction boundary. We will encapsulate the code that manages the transactional boundary in a class named *CommandExecutor*. Let's start with the tests that capture the requirements for the *CommandExecutor* class. We need to verify that the application code is executed. Here is the first test:

```
[TestFixture]
public class CommandExecutorFixture : ConnectionFixture
{
    private CommandExecutor commandExecutor =
        new CommandExecutor();

    private class ExecuteCommand : Command
    {
        internal int executeCount = 0;

        public void Execute()
        {
            executeCount++;
        }
    }

    [Test]
    public void RunOnce()
    {
        ExecuteCommand command = new ExecuteCommand();
        commandExecutor.Execute(command);
        Assert.AreEqual(1, command.executeCount);
    }
}
```

In this test, we introduce a couple of new classes. The first class is the *CommandExecutor*, which will eventually be responsible for running our application code within the context of a transaction. We also introduce an interface called *Command*, which is shown in the following code:

```
namespace DataAccess
{
    public interface Command
    {
```

```
      void Execute();
   }
}
```

We use *Command* (see *Design Patterns*, by Erich Gamma et al, Addison-Wesley, 1995) to encapsulate the application-specific code. The *Command-Executor* can then execute the command within the context of a transaction. The *Command* interface also allows us to better test the *CommandExecutor*. If you look at the *CommandExecutorFixture*, you see that we wrote a class named *ExecuteCommand*, which allows us to verify that the *Execute* method was called when it is run inside of the *CommandExecutor*. When we run the test, it passes, so let's move on to the more interesting parts such as the transaction boundary.

The next test will verify that when the *CommandExecutor* is called, it will start a transaction. Here is the test:

```
private class TransactionCheckCommand : Command
{
    internal SqlTransaction transaction;

    public void Execute()
    {
        transaction = TransactionManager.Transaction();
    }
}

[Test]
public void StartTransaction()
{
    TransactionCheckCommand command =
        new TransactionCheckCommand();
    commandExecutor.Execute(command);

    Assert.IsNotNull(command.transaction);
    Assert.IsNull(TransactionManager.Transaction());
}
```

This test uses another test command class named *TransactionCheck-Command*. All it does is record the transaction when the *Execute* method is called. When we run this test, it fails because the *command.transaction* is equal to *null*. This is not surprising because we have not put any database code (or transaction management code, for that matter) in the *Execute* method. Let's do that now.

```
public void Execute(Command command)
{
    bool isTransactionInProgress =
```

```
      (TransactionManager.Transaction() != null);

  if(!isTransactionInProgress)
  {
      SqlConnection connection = new SqlConnection(
        ConfigurationSettings.AppSettings.Get("Catalog.Connection"));
      connection.Open();
      TransactionManager.Begin(connection);
      command.Execute();
      TransactionManager.Commit();
      connection.Close();
  }
}
```

In this code, we open a connection to the database, start a transaction using the *TransactionManager*, execute the command in the context of the transaction, commit the transaction, and close the connection. When we run the tests in *CommandExecutorFixture* they all pass. Let's move on to the other scenario, in which the *CommandExecutor* needs to participate in a transaction that is already in progress. Here is the test:

```
[Test]
public void ParticipateInTransaction()
{
    SqlTransaction myTransaction = TransactionManager.Begin(Connection);
    TransactionCheckCommand command = new TransactionCheckCommand();
    commandExecutor.Execute(command);
    Assert.AreSame(myTransaction, command.transaction);
    TransactionManager.Rollback();
}
```

In this test, we start the transaction in the test and verify that the *CommandExecutor* uses the transaction. When we run the test, it fails. Let's fix the *CommandExecutor* to participate in transactions (the changes are in bold-face code):

```
public void Execute(Command command)
{
    bool isTransactionInProgress =
       (TransactionManager.Transaction() != null);

    if(isTransactionInProgress)
    {
        command.Execute();
    }
    else
    {
        SqlConnection connection = new SqlConnection(
```

```
    ConfigurationSettings.AppSettings.Get("Catalog.Connection"));
  connection.Open();

  TransactionManager.Begin(connection);
  command.Execute();
  TransactionManager.Commit();
  connection.Close();
  }
}
```

All we had to do in the participation case is call the *command.Execute* method. When we run the tests, they all pass.

The last test that we will show for the *CommandExecutor* is what should happen if the *Execute* method throws an exception. In this case, the *Command-Executor* should catch the exception, call the *TransactionManager.Rollback* to return the database to its previous state, and then rethrow the same exception so the calling program knows which exception was thrown. Here is the test in the *CommandExecutorFixture*:

```
private class ExceptionThrowingCommand : Command
{
  public void Execute()
  {
    throw new InvalidOperationException();
  }
}

[Test]
[ExpectedException(typeof(InvalidOperationException))]
public void ThrowCommand()
{
  ExceptionThrowingCommand command = new ExceptionThrowingCommand();
  commandExecutor.Execute(command);
}
```

Let's look at the implementation of the *CommandExecutor.Execute* method that's needed to support this test. The changes are boldface:

```
public void Execute(Command command)
{
  bool isTransactionInProgress =
    (TransactionManager.Transaction() != null);

  if(isTransactionInProgress)
  {
    command.Execute();
  }
  else
```

```
    {
        SqlConnection connection = new SqlConnection(
          ConfigurationSettings.AppSettings.Get("Catalog.Connection"));
        connection.Open();
        TransactionManager.Begin(connection);

        try
        {
          command.Execute();
          TransactionManager.Commit();
        }
        catch(Exception exception)
        {
          TransactionManager.Rollback();
          throw exception;
        }
        finally
        {
            connection.Close();
        }
    }
}
```

We had to do a little work on the code to catch the exception, call *Trans-action.Rollback*, and then rethrow the exception. We also had to ensure that we closed the connection to the database in either case. When we run the tests, they all pass as expected. There are a number of tests that need to be added to deal with the database-related exceptions, but we leave them as an exercise for the reader.

Now that we have implemented the generic *CommandExecutor* for the transactional execution of *Catalog* class' interface operations, we are ready to migrate the old code to the new execution strategy. Every interface method of the *Catalog* class will get converted following the same process described as follows:

- Create a private class in the *Catalog* class for the operation being performed (for example, *FindByRecordingIdCommand*).

- For each parameter of the original interface method, define an instance variable on the *Command* class and add it to the signature of the constructor.

- Define a property that will hold the return value of the original interface method.

- Define an *Execute* method that will have the same code as the original interface method.

- Replace the implementation of the original interface method with the construction and invocation of the corresponding command and use the *CommandExecutor*.

Here is the updated *Catalog* class for the *FindByRecordingId* method:

```
public class Catalog
{
    private static CommandExecutor commandExecutor =
        new CommandExecutor();

    private class FindByRecordingIdCommand : Command
    {
        internal long recordingId;
        internal RecordingDataSet recordingDataSet;
        internal RecordingDataSet.Recording recording;

        public FindByRecordingIdCommand(RecordingDataSet
            recordingDataSet, long recordingId)
        {
            this.recordingDataSet = recordingDataSet;
            this.recordingId = recordingId;
        }

        public void Execute()
        {
            SqlConnection connection =
            TransactionManager.Transaction().Connection;
            RecordingGateway recordingGateway =
                new RecordingGateway(connection);
            recording =
                recordingGateway.FindById(recordingId,
                    recordingDataSet);

            if(recording == null) return;

            long artistId = recording.ArtistId;
            ArtistGateway artistGateway = new
                ArtistGateway(connection);
            RecordingDataSet.Artist artist =
                artistGateway.FindById(artistId,
                    recordingDataSet);
```

```
long labelId = recording.LabelId;
LabelGateway labelGateway = new
    LabelGateway(connection);
RecordingDataSet.Label label =
    labelGateway.FindById(labelId,
        recordingDataSet);


GenreGateway genreGateway = new
    GenreGateway(connection);


TrackGateway trackGateway = new
    TrackGateway(connection);
foreach(RecordingDataSet.Track track in
    trackGateway.FindByRecordingId(recordingId,
        recordingDataSet))
{
    artistId = track.ArtistId;
    long genreId = track.GenreId;
    artist = artistGateway.FindById(artistId,
        recordingDataSet);
    RecordingDataSet.Genre genre =
        genreGateway.FindById(genreId,
            recordingDataSet);
}


ReviewGateway reviewGateway = new
ReviewGateway(connection);
ReviewerGateway reviewerGateway = new
    ReviewerGateway(connection);
foreach(RecordingDataSet.Review review in
    reviewGateway.FindByRecordingId(recordingId,
        recordingDataSet))
{
    long reviewerId = review.ReviewerId;

    RecordingDataSet.Reviewer reviewer =
        reviewerGateway.FindById(reviewerId,
            recordingDataSet);
}
}

public RecordingDataSet.Recording Result
{
    get
    {
        return recording;
    }
}
}
```

```
public static RecordingDataSet.Recording FindByRecordingId(
   RecordingDataSet recordingDataSet, long recordingId)
{
   FindByRecordingIdCommand command =
      new FindByRecordingIdCommand(recordingDataSet,
      recordingId);

   commandExecutor.Execute(command);
   return command.Result;
   }
}
```

After this work was completed, we ran the tests in the *CatalogFixture* and they passed. We then turned our attention to the *AddReview* and *DeleteReview* methods and followed exactly the same process. When we completed it, we ran all the tests and they passed. We removed the *[Ignore]* attribute from the *ReviewUpdateFixture*, ran those tests, and they passed as well. The last thing we did was run the customer tests, and they also passed. Having all the tests pass indicates that even though we made significant changes to the underlying implementation of the database access code, the application still works the same way as it did prior to these changes.

Summary

We started this chapter with the need to add transaction support to our application code to support the ease of writing programmer tests. With transaction support, we don't leave persistent garbage in the database. Changing to use transaction support at this point may seem like a lack of foresight on our part. However, if the customer decided not to provide Add/Delete Review functionality through the Web service, we would not have had to do this. It turns out, however, that using transactions simplified the programmer tests so much that we might be inclined to use this approach in the future, even if we did not have update functionality.

11

Service Layer Refactoring

In Chapter 10, "Programmer Tests: Using Transactions," we added support for transactions to our application. It was a significant architectural change that we made after a substantial part of the application had been built. In this chapter, we will implement another architectural refactoring that has to do with reorganizing the packaging of the application.

The Problem

In Chapter 12, "Implementing a Web Client," we will develop an ASP.NET Web client for the application. A typical enterprise application can have a variety of clients, and some of these clients provide interfaces for users to interact with the system; clients can also be in the form of other software systems consuming the services of the enterprise application. In both cases, the set of service operations provided by the enterprise application is conceptually shared among the clients. In the case of the application, we have a set of client-specific operations:

- Find a recording by *recordingId*

- Add a new review to an existing recording

- Delete a review from an existing recording

These operations are exposed to the single client of the application via the Web service. This client is another software system, or software systems that are likely to be hosted on a variety of technology platforms, which will be consuming the services of the application. This is why we chose to use Web services as the technology to expose the application's services.

Let's review the application architecture from the packaging perspective. Figure 11-1 shows what it looks like:

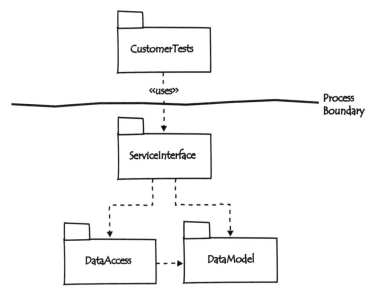

Figure 11-1   Application packages

There are several packages in the application:

■ **Data Access package**   This package is responsible for implementation of CRUD low-level operations for the underlying data in the data source. Data gateways (*RecordingGateway*, *LabelGateway*, and so on) are abstractions populating this package.

This package also has *TransactionManager* and its supporting classes (*Command* and *CommandExecutor*), defined here to make data gateways transaction-capable.

This package also has implemented application-specific transaction management and higher-level business operations. The *Catalog* class is another core abstraction in this package and it consolidates the CRUD operations into higher-level business operations.

■ **Data Model package**   This package defines a typed data set that establishes the data-level contract between the data source and the rest of the application. This contract is pretty low level and is tightly coupled to the database schema of the underlying data source. Although ADO.NET and the typed data set give a database-vendor independent views of the data, conceptually the two schemas—the data set and the database—are very tightly coupled and must be maintained together.

■ **Service Interface package**   To reduce the dependency between the data source's schema and the rest of the application, we have defined a Recording Data Transfer Object (DTO)—an XML representation of the data as viewed by the application. Recording DTO is the application-level representation of the data in the database, and this representation is captured by the *RecordingDto* class. This application-level contract hides some of the database-related specifics; for example, the database schema normalizations are not directly exposed on the Recording DTO; Artist, Label, Genre, and Reviewer are not represented as individual entities and are flattened to be simple string attributes on the corresponding objects (*Recording*, *Track*, and *Review*). We have created a *RecordingAssembler* class that is responsible for mapping between the two representations of the recording data.

This package also has *CatalogService* and *DatabaseCatalogService* classes that implement the functionality of retrieving the recording from the database and mapping it to the *RecordingDto* using the *RecordingAssembler*.

The Service Interface package hosts the *CatalogServiceInterface* class that exposes the application's operations as a Web service and adds mapping of the application exceptions into *SoapFaults* using the *ExceptionMapper* class.

The programmer tests are compiled into separate assemblies from the application code so that we can choose to deploy the code with or without the tests.

What's Wrong?

Let's take a closer look at the Service Interface package, which has classes that provide both a Web service-independent implementation of the application functionality and classes that are responsible for exposing and adapting this functionality via the Web service. The set of classes that are responsible for Web service–independent implementation of the application functionality includes *CatalogService*, *DatabaseCatalogService*, *RecordingDto*, and *RecordingAssembler*. This set of classes defines and implements a service-level contract between the application and its clients. We are adding a new client to the application, and this client needs to have access to this application-level contract.

Unfortunately, however, this contract is packaged with the Web service into one assembly.

We have also been putting off some cleanup for the programmer tests. We still have *StubCatalogService* and *StubCatalogServiceFixture* classes in our *service.interface.tests* assembly. These two classes do not add to the test coverage, and they complicate the application code.

The Solution

We will start by removing the stub implementation of the *CatalogService* and the corresponding programmer test. This change is very simple, and we can simply remove the two classes: *StubCatalogService* and *StubCatalogServiceFixture*.

The first change allows us to simplify the implementation of the *Catalog-Service* class. Now that we have just one implementation of the data retrieval strategy, we don't need to have the implementation span two classes: *Catalog-Service* and *DatabaseCatalogService*. These two classes can be merged into one (*CatalogService*), and we can get rid of the abstract methods and keep only the implementation. The following code shows what the new version of the *CatalogService* looks like:

```
using System;
using DataAccess;
using DataModel;

namespace ServiceInterface
{
    public class CatalogService
    {
        public RecordingDto FindByRecordingId(long id)
        {
            RecordingDataSet dataSet = new RecordingDataSet();
            RecordingDataSet.Recording recording =
                Catalog.FindByRecordingId(dataSet, id);

            if(recording == null) return null;

            return RecordingAssembler.WriteDto(recording);
        }

        public ReviewDto AddReview(string reviewerName, string content,
            int rating, long recordingId)
        {
            RecordingDataSet dataSet = new RecordingDataSet();
            RecordingDataSet.Review review =
                Catalog.AddReview(dataSet, reviewerName, content,
                    rating, recordingId);
```

```
        return RecordingAssembler.WriteReview(review);
    }

    public void DeleteReview(long reviewId)
    {
        Catalog.DeleteReview(reviewId);
    }
  }
}
```

To do part of this refactoring, we had to change the users of the old *CatalogService* and *DatabaseCatalogService* classes.

The next step is to split the Service Interface package into two:

■   First, the package responsible for exposing the application's operations using the Web services; we keep the name as the Service Interface package

■   Second, the package that actually defines the application services in a way that is independent of which client uses it; we call it the Service Layer

As part of this split, we need to restructure a few other packages. The mechanics of this refactoring are not complex. We will define a separate namespace, *ServiceLayer*, to host the classes of the Service Layer. We need to move the classes that define the application-level data contract and the classes that are responsible for the implementation of this contract into the *ServiceLayer* namespace. These classes are as follows:

■   *RecordingDto* generated from *RecordingDto* schema

■   *RecordingAssembler*

■   *CatalogService*

We will also move the related programmer test fixtures into this new namespace. The following test classes will be moved to this namespace:

■   *CatalogServiceFixture* (this class was called *DatabaseCatalogServiceFixture* before we rolled up the *CatalogService* and *DatabaseCatalogService* into one class: *CatalogService*)

■   *DatabaseUpdateReviewFixture*

■   *InMemoryRecordingBuilder*

■   *RecordingAssemblerFixture*, *ReviewAssemblerFixture*, and *TrackAssemblerFixture*

Modern refactoring tools support such refactoring, and they make it much easier to handle a task like this for much larger applications, in which thousands of classes might need to be moved. However, we do not have one of those tools, so we need to do this manually. When we get everything to compile again, we rerun all the tests, and they pass.

We are almost finished. We have one undesirable package dependency still present. The *ExistingReviewMapper* class from the *ServiceInterface* package needs to have access to the *ExistingReviewException* class defined in the *DataAccess* package. We want to break that dependency by moving the *ExistingReviewException* into a new package: *ServerExceptions*.

Figure 11-2 shows what our application architecture looks like after the extraction of the Service Layer.

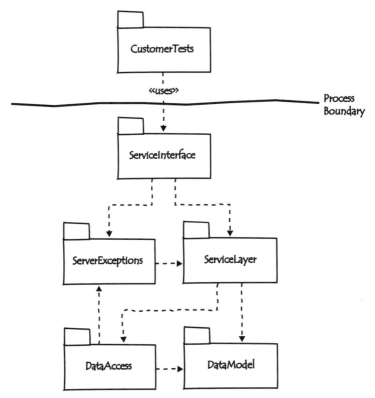

Figure 11-2   Application architecture after *ServiceLayer* refactoring

Summary

In this chapter, we completed another architectural refactoring. We extracted the application operations into a separate package; we did not need this package until we came to the point of writing the second client for our application. The need to share the code between the clients was the major driving force behind this refactoring.

As is often the case with software development, the system's original design does not stay unchanged because the requirements evolve and the system's structure must follow the same evolution process.

12

Implementing a Web Client

In this last chapter, we will start the implementation of a Web client. In its final form, the Web client will allow users to search for recording information stored in the database, modify the various attributes of a recording, and delete questionable reviews.

This chapter shows the implementation of the Search page, which demonstrates many of the issues you might encounter when developing a Web client using Test-Driven Development.

Testing User Interfaces

Testing user interface code challenges you in a number of ways differently than testing situations we have described previously.

- **Functional testing**   The easiest way to test a Web application is to open a Web browser, type in the URL, and verify that the Web page works as expected. This process can be automated with tools that simulate user inputs and then verify that the page returned has the expected values. The Microsoft Application Center Test tool is one example. There is nothing wrong with these types of tests; the issue with regard to TDD is that we need a way to incrementally build the system with programmer tests.

- **Programmer tests in ASP.NET**   What we want to do is instantiate a page object inside an NUnit test and then test it as we would any other object. It turns out that you can instantiate the page objects in the test, but they aren't instantiated the same way as is done by *HttpRuntime*. For example, none of the controls is initialized when you instantiate the page in the test. You can manually instantiate them, but you have to ask yourself what you are testing at this point. You could decide to host the *HttpRuntime*, which is possible, but has it own troubles. (For a detailed discussion of how to do this, along with sample code, see *http://hyperthink.net/blog/permalink.aspx?guid=271632d2-07e3-41af-9e58-9a7e25348b8c*.) Because we can't do what we want to do directly, we'll build as much functionality as possible outside of ASP.NET instead in order to be able to write programmer tests.

By the end of this chapter, you should have a good understanding of the issues associated with writing programmer tests for Web-based user interfaces and how some of these issues are mitigated using the testing strategies presented here.

The Task

The part of the Web client that we are building in this chapter is a Search page. The user enters search criteria and pushes a button, and the system retrieves a list of recordings that match the search criteria. The search criterion includes the Id (which returns only a single recording), Artist Name, Title, Average Rating, and Label Name (all of which can return multiple recordings).

When the user pushes the Search button, the system should retrieve the recordings that match the criteria and display them in a tabular form. Each row of the table will display a recording that matches the search criteria. The columns to be displayed are the Title, Artist Name, Average Rating, and the Label Name. A sketch of the screen is shown in Figure 12-1.

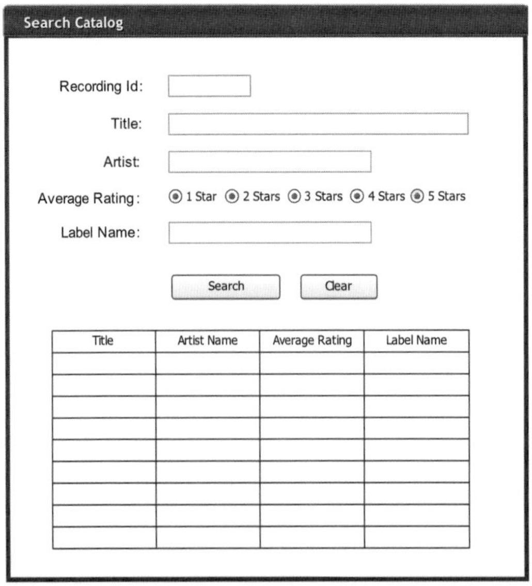

Figure 12-1 The Search page

Implementing Search

It looks as if we need to have a page in which the user enters search criteria and then pushes the Search button. When the Search button is pushed, we need to copy the criteria from the page and pass it to a method in the *CatalogService* class, which will search the database, using the criteria, and return an *ArrayList* of recordings that match the search criteria. When we get the *ArrayList* back, we will have to bind it to a *Repeater* to have the results displayed in the tabular form.

This implementation is really two separate tasks: the first task is to implement the search functionality in the *CatalogService* class, and the second task is to write the Web page that interacts with the user and calls the method in the *CatalogService* to retrieve the results. Separating the tasks allows us to implement the majority of the implementation (the *CatalogService* search method) using the same techniques we used in previous chapters.

Implementing the Search Service

The existing *CatalogService* class does not provide a method to search the recording database. We implemented this functionality using the techniques we demonstrated in the previous chapters, but we do not show the step-by-step implementation here. (The completed functionality with programmer and customer tests is available in the companion website that we mentioned in the Introduction.) The steps were not much different from what we did for other *CatalogService* methods, such as *FindByRecordingId*, *AddReview*, and *DeleteReview*.

Here is the *Search* method implementation in the *CatalogService* class:

```
public ArrayList Search(SearchCriteria criteria)
{
    ArrayList searchResults = new ArrayList();

    ArrayList recordings = Catalog.Search(criteria);
    foreach(RecordingDataSet.Recording recording in recordings)
    {
        searchResults.Add(RecordingAssembler.WriteDto(recording));
    }

    return searchResults;
}
```

SearchCriteria is defined as follows:

```
public struct SearchCriteria
{
    public long id;
    public string artistName;
```

```
        public string title;
        public string labelName;
        public int averageRating;
    }
```

Implementing the Search Page

Now that the *CatalogService* task is complete, we can focus entirely on the Web application code. Just as we did in Chapter 6, "Programmer Tests: Using TDD with ASP.NET Web Services," we will isolate the code we are working on (Web application code) from the underlying implementation (*CatalogService*) by implementing the *CatalogServiceStub*.

Here is the first test:

```
[TestFixture]
public class SearchFixture
{
    [Test]
    public void SearchById()
    {
        SearchCriteria criteria = new SearchCriteria();
        criteria.id = 42;

        CatalogServiceStub serviceStub = new CatalogServiceStub();
        ArrayList results = serviceStub.Search(criteria);

        Assert.AreEqual(1, results.Count);

        RecordingDto dto = (RecordingDto)results[0];
        Assert.AreEqual(criteria.id, dto.id);
    }
}
```

This test specifies the need for a *CatalogServiceStub* class with a method named *Search*, which takes as input the *SearchCriteria* class and returns an *ArrayList* of *RecordingDto* objects that match the criteria. The test verifies that the method returns a single *RecordingDto* and that the *RecordingDto.id* is equal to the value that we specified in the search criteria. Here is the implementation of *CatalogServiceStub* that will make the test pass:

```
public class CatalogServiceStub
{
    public ArrayList Search(SearchCriteria criteria)
    {
        ArrayList results = new ArrayList();

        RecordingDto dto = new RecordingDto();
        dto.id = criteria.id;
```

```
    results.Add(dto);
    return results;
    }
}
```

This implementation is an example of the technique called "Fake It ('Til You Make It)" described in *Test-Driven Development* by Kent Beck (Addison-Wesley, 2003). We are faking the call to *CatalogService* and returning a known value. Let's write another test that expects multiple *RecordingDto* objects.

```
[Test]
public void SearchByArtistName()
{
    SearchCriteria criteria = new SearchCriteria();
    criteria.artistName = "Fake Artist Name";

    CatalogServiceStub serviceStub = new CatalogServiceStub();
    ArrayList results = serviceStub.Search(criteria);

    Assert.AreEqual(2, results.Count);

    foreach(RecordingDto dto in results)
        Assert.AreEqual(criteria.artistName, dto.artistName);
}
```

This test states that if we specify the *artistName* criteria, we'll get two *RecordingDto* objects back, and the *RecordingDto.artistName* field will be equal to the value we specified in the criteria. Here is the *CatalogServiceStub* implementation:

```
public ArrayList Search(SearchCriteria criteria)
{
    ArrayList results = new ArrayList();

    if(criteria.id != 0)
    {
        RecordingDto dto = new RecordingDto();
        dto.id = criteria.id;

        results.Add(dto);
    }
    else if(criteria.artistName != null)
    {
        RecordingDto dto = new RecordingDto();
        dto.artistName = criteria.artistName;
        results.Add(dto);
        results.Add(dto);
    }
```

```
    return results;
  }
```

The implementation of the *CatalogServiceStub* is not very sophisticated because it does not have to be. The goal is to simulate a couple of scenarios, and this is sufficient.

Binding the Results to a *Repeater* Web Control

The task description states that we have to bind the search results to a *Repeater* Web control. The data source for the *Repeater* can be anything that implements the *IEnumerable* interface. Because *ArrayList* does implement *IEnumerable*, we don't have any problem with that. However, we can't use the *RecordingDto* class as the item in the *ArrayList* because the *Repeater* Web control has to bind to public property fields on the object, and the *RecordingDto* has public member variables—not properties. Because the *RecordingDto* is generated using xsd.exe, we need to create another object to adapt the *RecordingDto* to something that can be used by the *Repeater* Web control. We will call this class the *RecordingDisplayAdapter*, and its responsibility will be to provide public properties for the fields that will be displayed onscreen.

Here are the tests:

```
[TestFixture]
public class RecordingDisplayAdapterFixture
{
    private RecordingDto dto = new RecordingDto();
    private RecordingDisplayAdapter adapter;

    [SetUp]
    public void SetUp()
    {
        dto.id = 42;
        dto.title = "Fake Title";
        dto.labelName = "Fake Label Name";
        dto.artistName = "Fake Artist Name";
        dto.averageRating = 5;

        adapter = new RecordingDisplayAdapter(dto);
    }

    [Test]
    public void VerifyTitle()
    {
        Assert.AreEqual(dto.title, adapter.Title);
    }
```

```
[Test]
public void VerifyArtistName()
{
    Assert.AreEqual(dto.artistName, adapter.ArtistName);
}

[Test]
public void VerifyAverageRating()
{
    Assert.AreEqual(dto.averageRating, adapter.AverageRating);
}

[Test]
public void VerifyId()
{
    Assert.AreEqual(dto.id, adapter.Id);
}

[Test]
public void VerifyLabelName()
{
    Assert.AreEqual(dto.labelName, adapter.LabelName);
}
}
```

The resulting implementation of *RecordingDisplayAdapter* is as follows:

```
public class RecordingDisplayAdapter
{
    private RecordingDto dto;

    public RecordingDisplayAdapter(RecordingDto dto)
    {
        this.dto = dto;
    }

    public string Title
    {
        get { return dto.title; }
    }

    public string ArtistName
    {
        get { return dto.artistName; }
    }

    public string LabelName
```

```
{
    get { return dto.labelName; }
}

public int AverageRating
{
    get { return dto.averageRating; }
}

public long Id
{
    get { return dto.id; }
}
}
```

RecordingDisplayAdapter is an example of a design pattern called Adapter.[1] It has a single responsibility: to adapt the *RecordingDto* so it can be bound to the *Repeater* Web control. Now we need to convert the list of *RecordingDto* objects that we get back from the *CatalogServiceStub* into a list of *RecordingDisplayAdapter* objects. Let's modify the *SearchFixture* tests to expect a list of *RecordingDisplayAdapter* objects instead of *RecordingDto* objects.

Here are the tests with the changes in boldface:

```
[TestFixture]
public class SearchFixture
{
    [Test]
    public void SearchById()
    {
        SearchCriteria criteria = new SearchCriteria();
        criteria.id = 42;

        CatalogServiceGateway gateway =
            new CatalogServiceGateway();
        ArrayList results = gateway.Search(criteria);

        Assert.AreEqual(1, results.Count);

        RecordingDisplayAdapter adapter =
            (RecordingDisplayAdapter)results[0];
        Assert.AreEqual(criteria.id, adapter.Id);
    }

    [Test]
    public void SearchByArtistName()
```

---

1. E. Gamma, et al. *Design Patterns*, Addison-Wesley, 1995.

```
    {
        SearchCriteria criteria = new SearchCriteria();
        criteria.artistName = "Fake Artist Name";

        CatalogServiceGateway gateway =
            new CatalogServiceGateway();
        ArrayList results = gateway.Search(criteria);

        Assert.AreEqual(2, results.Count);

        foreach(RecordingDisplayAdapter adapter in results)
            Assert.AreEqual(criteria.artistName, adapter.ArtistName);
    }
}
```

Because the *CatalogServiceStub* returns a list of *RecordingDto* objects, we have to introduce another class, *CatalogServiceGateway*, whose responsibility is to call the *CatalogServiceStub* to retrieve the list of *RecordingDto* objects and turn it into a list of *RecordingDisplayAdapter* objects.

Here is the *CatalogServiceGateway* class that makes the tests pass:

```
public class CatalogServiceGateway
{
    public ArrayList Search(SearchCriteria criteria)
    {
        ArrayList results = new ArrayList();

        CatalogServiceStub stub = new CatalogServiceStub();
        ArrayList dtos = stub.Search(criteria);

        foreach(RecordingDto dto in dtos)
        {
            RecordingDisplayAdapter adapter =
                new RecordingDisplayAdapter(dto);
            results.Add(adapter);
        }

        return results;
    }
}
```

When we compile and run the tests, they all pass, so we can move on.

Creating the Page

You might wonder when we will actually write the page. What we have done so far is to implement the functionality that the page uses in a testable way.

Now we need to write the page that uses this tested functionality. We use the tools in Visual Studio to lay out the page.

The following is the code-behind page that Visual Studio creates:

```
public class SearchPage : System.Web.UI.Page
{
    protected System.Web.UI.WebControls.Label idLabel;
    protected System.Web.UI.WebControls.Label titleLabel;
    protected System.Web.UI.WebControls.Label artistNameLabel;
    protected System.Web.UI.WebControls.Label averageRatingLabel;
    protected System.Web.UI.WebControls.Label labelNameLabel;
    protected System.Web.UI.WebControls.TextBox recordingId;
    protected System.Web.UI.WebControls.TextBox title;
    protected System.Web.UI.WebControls.TextBox artistName;
    protected System.Web.UI.WebControls.TextBox labelName;
    protected System.Web.UI.WebControls.RadioButtonList averageRating;
    protected System.Web.UI.WebControls.Button searchButton;
    protected System.Web.UI.WebControls.Button cancelButton;
    protected System.Web.UI.WebControls.Repeater searchResults;

    private void Page_Load(object sender, System.EventArgs e)
    {
        // Put user code to initialize the page here
    }

    // Web Form Designer generated code

    private void SearchButtonClick(object sender, System.EventArgs e)
    {
    }
}
```

We compile this page and then display the page in the browser. The page displays correctly, but when we push the Search button, nothing happens because we have not written it yet. Let's correct that by writing the *SearchButtonClick* method by just using the *recordingId* field:

```
private void SearchButtonClick(object sender, System.EventArgs e)
{
    long idValue = Int64.Parse(recordingId.Text);

    SearchCriteria criteria = new SearchCriteria();
    criteria.id = idValue;

    searchResults.DataSource = gateway.Search(criteria);
    searchResults.DataBind();
}
```

This method is responsible for translating the text box fields onscreen into the *SearchCriteria* class and then calling the *CatalogServiceGateway* to get the results. We hope it feels strange that we did not implement a test before we wrote this code. We had to do it because there is no way to write this test within the context of ASP.NET. However, we can separate this translation code into a helper class and test this helper class outside the context of ASP.NET.

Here are the tests:

```
[TestFixture]
public class SearchPageHelperFixture
{
   private static readonly string idText = "42";
   private static readonly string titleText = "Fake Title";
   private static readonly string artistNameText = "Fake Artist Name";
   private static readonly string averageRating = "3";
   private static readonly string labelText = "Fake Label Name";

   private SearchCriteria criteria;
   private SearchPageHelper helper = new SearchPageHelper();

   [SetUp]
   public void SetUp()
   {
      criteria = helper.Translate(
         idText, titleText, artistNameText, averageRating,
         labelText);
   }

   [Test]
   public void VerifyId()
   {
      Assert.AreEqual(Int64.Parse(idText), criteria.id);
   }

   [Test]
   public void VerifyTitle()
   {
      Assert.AreEqual(titleText, criteria.title);
   }

   [Test]
   public void VerifyLabel()
   {
      Assert.AreEqual(labelText, criteria.labelName);
   }

   [Test]
```

```
public void VerifyArtistName()
{
    Assert.AreEqual(artistNameText, criteria.artistName);
}

[Test]
public void VerifyAverageRating()
{
    Assert.AreEqual(Int32.Parse(averageRating),
            criteria.averageRating);
}
}
```

The *SearchPageHelper* implementation is as follows:

```
public class SearchPageHelper
{
    public SearchCriteria Translate(
        string id, string title, string artistName,
        string averageRating, string labelName)
    {
        SearchCriteria criteria = new SearchCriteria();

        criteria.id = Int64.Parse(id);
        criteria.title = title;
        criteria.labelName = labelName;
        criteria.artistName = artistName;
        criteria.averageRating = Int32.Parse(averageRating);

        return criteria;
    }
}
```

What we did is split out code that is usually done in the code-behind page into a separate class that does the translation so that we can test it. Let's modify the *SearchButtonClick* method to use the newly created *SearchPageHelper* class:

```
private void SearchButtonClick(object sender, System.EventArgs e)
{
    SearchCriteria criteria = helper.Translate(
        recordingId.Text, title.Text, artistName.Text,
        averageRating.SelectedValue, labelName.Text);

    searchResults.DataSource = gateway.Search(criteria);
    searchResults.DataBind();
}
```

When we open the browser to test the page, it works correctly, but we have to put values in the *recordingId* field and select one of the average rating radio buttons. If we do not put values in the *recordingId* field or fail to select one of the average rating radio buttons, the page fails because we cannot parse the text fields into numbers. Let's add some tests in the *SearchPageHelper-Fixture* class that captures these requirements:

```
[Test]
public void IdFieldNotSpecified()
{
   criteria = helper.Translate(
      null, titleText, artistNameText, averageRating, labelText);
   Assert.AreEqual(0, criteria.id);
}

[Test]
public void AverageRatingFieldNotSpecified()
{
   criteria = helper.Translate(
      null, titleText, artistNameText, null, labelText);
   Assert.AreEqual(0, criteria.averageRating);
}
```

The corresponding change to the *SearchPageHelper* class is in boldface in the following code:

```
public class SearchPageHelper
{
   public SearchCriteria Translate(
      string id, string title, string artistName,
      string averageRating, string labelName)
   {
      SearchCriteria criteria = new SearchCriteria();

      try
      {
         criteria.id = Int64.Parse(id);
      }
      catch(Exception)
      {
         criteria.id = 0;
      }

      criteria.title = title;
      criteria.labelName = labelName;
      criteria.artistName = artistName;

      try
      {
         criteria.averageRating = Int32.Parse(averageRating);
```

```
        }
        catch(Exception)
        {
            criteria.averageRating = 0;
        }

        return criteria;
    }
}
```

When we look at the code in the *SearchButtonClick* method, we see that there isn't anything else we can extract from this method to write programmer tests because the rest of the code depends on the ASP.NET environment. What we have done, though, is make the code that is not testable with NUnit as small as possible. We will have to test the rest manually with the browser or use a testing tool that simulates the browser environment.

Enough of This Stub

The code that we implemented uses the *CatalogServiceStub*. It's about time to see whether the code will work with the real service layer implementation. Looking at the implementation of the *CatalogServiceGateway*, you will see that it is hard-wired to use the *CatalogServiceStub*. We need a way to specify the *CatalogServiceStub* when we execute the programmer tests and another class that calls the real *CatalogService* when we execute the customer tests.

The current implementation of *CatalogServiceGateway* is as follows:

```
public class CatalogServiceGateway
{
    public ArrayList Search(SearchCriteria criteria)
    {
        ArrayList results = new ArrayList();

        CatalogServiceStub stub = new CatalogServiceStub();
        ArrayList dtos = stub.Search(criteria);

        foreach(RecordingDto dto in dtos)
        {
            RecordingDisplayAdapter adapter =
                new RecordingDisplayAdapter(dto);
            results.Add(adapter);
        }

        return results;
    }
}
```

Clearly, we can't have this class instantiate the *CatalogServiceStub*. So how can we make this switch invisible to the code in the *SearchPage.aspx.cs*? The simplest way to do this is to have the *CatalogServiceGateway* class defer the retrieval of the search results to a derived class. The changes are in boldface:

```
public abstract class CatalogServiceGateway
{
    public ArrayList Search(SearchCriteria criteria)
    {
        ArrayList results = new ArrayList();

        ArrayList dtos = GetDtos(criteria);
        foreach(RecordingDto dto in dtos)
        {
            RecordingDisplayAdapter adapter =
                new RecordingDisplayAdapter(dto);
            results.Add(adapter);
        }

        return results;
    }

    protected abstract ArrayList GetDtos(SearchCriteria criteria);
}
```

Now, derived classes will have to implement the *GetDtos* method. When we try to compile it, it fails because *CatalogServiceGateway* is an abstract class and can no longer be instantiated. We need to modify the *CatalogServiceStub* to inherit from *CatalogServiceGateway* to implement the *GetDtos* method for the tests.

Here is the updated version with the changes in boldface:

```
public class CatalogServiceStub : CatalogServiceGateway
{
    protected override ArrayList GetDtos(SearchCriteria criteria)
    {
        ArrayList results = new ArrayList();

        if(criteria.id != 0)
        {
            RecordingDto dto = new RecordingDto();
            dto.id = criteria.id;

            results.Add(dto);
        }
        else if(criteria.artistName != null)
        {
```

```
        RecordingDto dto = new RecordingDto();
        dto.artistName = criteria.artistName;
        results.Add(dto);
        results.Add(dto);
      }

      return results;
   }
}
```

When this change is made, the *SearchFixture* tests no longer compile because they try to instantiate the *CatalogServiceGateway*. The changes are in boldface in the following code:

```
[TestFixture]
public class SearchFixture
{
   [Test]
   public void SearchById()
   {
      SearchCriteria criteria = new SearchCriteria();
      criteria.id = 42;

      CatalogServiceStub stub = new CatalogServiceStub();
      ArrayList results = stub.Search(criteria);

      Assert.AreEqual(1, results.Count);

      RecordingDisplayAdapter adapter =
         (RecordingDisplayAdapter)results[0];
      Assert.AreEqual(criteria.id, adapter.Id);
   }

   [Test]
   public void SearchByArtistName()
   {
      SearchCriteria criteria = new SearchCriteria();
      criteria.artistName = "Fake Artist Name";

      CatalogServiceStub stub = new CatalogServiceStub();
      ArrayList results = stub.Search(criteria);

      Assert.AreEqual(2, results.Count);

      foreach(RecordingDisplayAdapter adapter in results)
         Assert.AreEqual(criteria.artistName, adapter.ArtistName);
   }
}
```

The last change we need to make is to the *SearchPage.aspx.cs* class; we will change *CatalogServiceGateway* to *CatalogServiceStub* so that the page will compile. The program now works as it did before we started making this change. Now that we have the code back to a stable state, we can implement another class that derives from *CatalogServiceGateway* and makes the real call to the *CatalogService*.

Here is the *CatalogServiceImplementation* class:

```
public class CatalogServiceImplementation : CatalogServiceGateway
{
    private CatalogService service = new CatalogService();

    protected override ArrayList GetDtos(SearchCriteria criteria)
    {
        return service.Search(criteria);
    }
}
```

After this code compiles, we can change the *SearchPage.aspx.cs* class to instantiate the *CatalogServiceImplementation* class, and the Web page will use the *CatalogService* class in the service layer and search the database. The following is the updated *SearchPage.aspx.cs* class with the change in boldface:

```
public class SearchPage : System.Web.UI.Page
{
    protected System.Web.UI.WebControls.Label idLabel;
    protected System.Web.UI.WebControls.Label titleLabel;
    protected System.Web.UI.WebControls.Label artistNameLabel;
    protected System.Web.UI.WebControls.Label averageRatingLabel;
    protected System.Web.UI.WebControls.Label labelNameLabel;
    protected System.Web.UI.WebControls.TextBox recordingId;
    protected System.Web.UI.WebControls.TextBox title;
    protected System.Web.UI.WebControls.TextBox artistName;
    protected System.Web.UI.WebControls.TextBox labelName;
    protected System.Web.UI.WebControls.RadioButtonList averageRating;
    protected System.Web.UI.WebControls.Button searchButton;
    protected System.Web.UI.WebControls.Button cancelButton;
    protected System.Web.UI.WebControls.Repeater searchResults;

    private CatalogServiceGateway gateway =
        new CatalogServiceImplementation();
    private SearchPageHelper helper = new SearchPageHelper();

    private void Page_Load(object sender, System.EventArgs e)
    {
        // Put user code to initialize the page here
    }
```

```
// Web Form Designer generated code


private void SearchButtonClick(object sender, System.EventArgs e)
{
    SearchCriteria criteria = helper.Translate(
        recordingId.Text, title.Text, artistName.Text,
        averageRating.SelectedValue, labelName.Text);

    searchResults.DataSource = gateway.Search(criteria);
    searchResults.DataBind();
}
}
```

When we recompile and bring the page up in the browser, we can search the database using the *SearchPage*.

Summary

Testing user interfaces can be challenging and often requires a bit more test scaffolding, as demonstrated in this example. However, the more code you can make testable, the more reliable the system will be. We could have taken the approach of traditional user interface testing mechanisms, but (as stated in the beginning of this chapter) most of them do not allow the incremental development style that we advocate here.

The approach outlined in this chapter builds most of the functionality outside the context of the user interface code, and we hook it up to the user interface only after the majority of the code is built. The approach used in this chapter yields user interface code that is just a thin layer on top of rigorously tested code.

Part III

Appendixes

Appendix A

NUnit Primer

In Chapter 1, "Test-Driven Development Practices," we discussed the need for a framework to support the development, management, and execution of automated programmer tests. In this appendix, we introduce NUnit, which is a testing framework for all Microsoft .NET programming languages. Initially ported from JUnit, the current version (2.1.4) is written entirely in C# and has been completely redesigned to take advantage of many .NET language features—for example, custom attributes and other reflection-related capabilities.

To demonstrate NUnit's capabilities, we will start with a very simple example: adding two integer numbers.

NUnit Quick Start

The initial step, if you have not taken it already, is to download NUnit from *www.nunit.org*. The file, NUnit.msi, is a Microsoft Windows Installation file. After downloading the installation program, double-click the file to start the installation procedure. The installation program suggests that the program be installed into C:\Program Files\NUnit V2.1. In most cases, the default directory is adequate.

Step 1. Create Visual Studio Project for your test code.

Let's start by creating a new project in Microsoft Visual Studio .NET. Select Visual C# Projects as the type of project and Class Library as the template. Name the project *NUnitQuickStart*. Figure A-1 is a Visual Studio .NET screen shot that demonstrates this step:

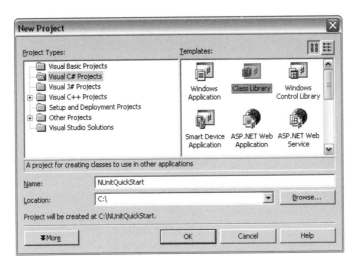

Figure A-1   Creating the first NUnit project

Step 2. Add a reference to the NUnit Framework.

When building this example in Microsoft Visual Studio .NET, you'll need to add a reference to the *nunit.framework.dll*, as follows:

1.   Right-click the References folder in the Solution Explorer and select Add Reference.

2.   Select the nunit.framework component from the .NET tab and press the Select and OK buttons in the Add Reference dialog box.

Figure A-2 demonstrates this step:

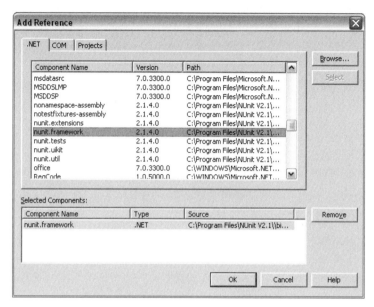

Figure A-2   Adding a reference to *nunit.framework.dll* to the project

Step 3. Add a class to the project.

Add the *NumbersFixture* class to the project. Here's the code for this example:

```
using System;
using NUnit.Framework;

namespace NUnitQuickStart
{
    [TestFixture]
    public class NumbersFixture
    {
        [Test]
        public void AddTwoNumbers()
        {
            int a = 1;
            int b = 2;
            int sum = a + b;
            Assert.AreEqual(3, sum);
        }
    }
}
```

Step 4. Set up your Visual Studio Project to use the NUnit-Gui test runner.

To automatically run the NUnit-Gui test runner from within Visual Studio .NET, you need to set up NUnit-Gui as your startup application. Here's how to do it:

1. Right-click your *NUnitQuickStart* project in the Solution Explorer.

2. Select Properties from the context menu.

3. Click the Configuration Properties folder in the left panel of the dialog box that displays.

4. Select Debugging from the list that appears under the Configuration Properties folder.

5. In the Start Action section on the right side of the Properties dialog box, choose Program from the drop-down box as the value for Debug Mode.

6. Press the Apply button.

7. Set **nunit-gui.exe** to be the Start Application. You can either type in the full path to nunit-gui.exe or use the browse button to navigate to it. (The default location is C:\Program Files\NUnit V2.1\bin\.)

Figure A-3 helps to demonstrate this step:

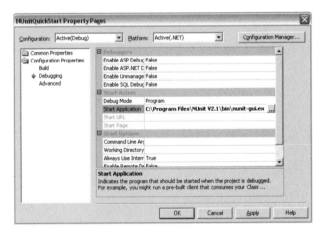

Figure A-3   Setting up NUnit-Gui as the test runner for the project

Step 5. Compile and run your test.

Now build the solution. After it is successfully compiled, start the application; the NUnit-Gui test runner appears. When you start NUnit-Gui for the first time, it opens with no tests loaded. Select Open from the File menu and browse to the location of *NUnitQuickStart.dll*. When you load the assembly with tests, the test runner creates a visual representation of the tests packaged in the loaded assembly. In the example, the test assembly has only one test, and the test assembly's structure looks something like that shown in Figure A-4.

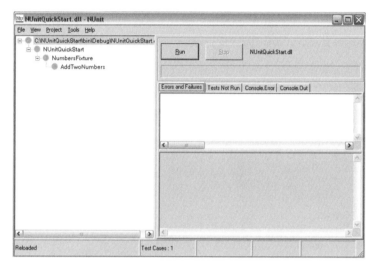

Figure A-4   Visual representation of tests from the NUnitQuickStart test assembly in the NUnit-Gui test runner

Click the Run button. The tree nodes turn green, and the progress bar in the test runner window turns green. Green indicates success!

Step 6. Become familiar with the NUnit-Gui layout.

Let's take a closer look at the layout of the test runner window. In the center of the right panel, you'll see a test progress bar. The color of this bar reflects the status of the test's execution:

- **Green**   indicates that all the tests executed so far are successful.
- **Yellow**   means that some tests are ignored but there are no failures.
- **Red**   signals that there are failures.

A status bar at the bottom shows the following panels:

■ **Status** shows the current status of the tests being run. When all tests finish, the status changes to *Completed*. During the running of the tests, the status shows *Running: <test-name>* where *<test-name>* is the name of the current test being run.

■ **Test Cases** shows the total count of test cases found in the loaded assembly. Note that this is the number of leaf nodes in the test tree. (*Leaf nodes* are nodes without descendants.)

■ **Tests Run** shows a running count of tests that have been completed.

■ **Failures** shows a running count of all tests that have failed so far.

■ **Time** displays how long it took to run the tests (time is displayed in seconds).

The main File menu has the following contents:

■ **New Project** allows you to create a new project. A project is a collection of test assemblies; this mechanism lets you organize tests from multiple test assemblies and treat them as a group.

■ **Open** loads a new test assembly or a previously saved NUnit project file.

■ **Close** closes the currently loaded test assembly or currently loaded NUnit project.

■ **Save** lets you save the current NUnit project in a file; if you're working with a single assembly, this menu item allows you to create a new NUnit project and save it in a file.

■ **Save As** allows you to save the current NUnit project as a file.

■ **Reload** forces a reload of the current test assembly or the NUnit project; the NUnit-Gui automatically watches for changes to the currently loaded test assemblies.

   When the assembly changes, the test runner reloads the test assembly. (The currently loaded test assembly is not reloaded while the tests are being run; the test assembly can be reloaded only between the test runs.) There is one caveat: if the test assembly depends on other assemblies, the test runner does not see changes to any dependant assemblies. Forcing a reload makes all dependent assembly changes visible to the test runner, as well.

- **Recent Files**   shows the history of the five most recent test assemblies or NUnit projects loaded in the test runner (this list is kept in the Windows registry and is maintained per user, so you see your tests only if you share your PC). The number of recent assemblies can be changed using the Options menu item, accessible from the main Tool menu.

- **Exit**   leaves the program.

The View menu has the following contents:

- **Expand**   expands the currently selected node in the tree by one level.

- **Collapse**   collapses the currently selected node in the tree.

- **Expand All**   recursively expands all nodes in the tree that are below the currently selected node.

- **Collapse All**   recursively collapses all nodes in the tree that are below the currently selected node.

- **Expand Fixtures**   expands all nodes in the tree that represent test fixtures.

- **Collapse Fixtures**   collapses all nodes in the tree that represent test fixtures.

- **Properties**   opens the dialog box that displays the properties of the currently selected node in the tree.

The Tools menu has these items:

- **Save Results as XML**   saves the most recent results of running the tests as an XML file.

- **Options**   lets you customize some of the NUnit test runner behavior.

Now let's have a look at the right panel. You are already familiar with the Run button and the progress bar. There is also a Stop button next to the Run button: clicking this button terminates the execution of the tests being run. Below the progress bar is a text window with the following four tabs above it:

- **The Errors and Failures**   window shows the tests that did not pass. In our case, this window is empty.

- **The Tests Not Run**   window shows the tests that did not get executed.

- **The Console.Error** window shows the error messages that the running tests produced. These are the messages that an application code can output using the *Console.Error* output stream.

- **The Console.Out** window shows text messages printed by the running tests to the *Console.Out* output stream.

NUnit Core Concepts

Now that you have successfully coded, compiled, and executed your first programmer tests, let's spend some time exploring the vocabulary of the NUnit Framework. So far, we have talked about test fixtures, test cases, and test runners. In the following section, we discuss test case.

Test Case

Test case is a self-validating programmer test that can be automatically discovered and executed independently of other test cases by a test runner. Following are a few important points about test case:

- Test case is a *programmer test*. Although it is a pretty loose concept to pin down, the general rule of thumb is that the programmer test is a low-level test that aims to verify either method-level or class-level behavior.

- Test case is a *self-validating test*, which means that each programmer test has a built-in mechanism to verify and report its success or failure status. A self-validating test does not require human intervention or interpretation.

- Test case can be *automatically discovered* by a test runner, which implies that there should be a mechanism in place to unambiguously identify test cases to a test runner.

- Test case can be *automatically executed* by a test runner. Again, this means that there should be no human intervention required to complete execution of a test case. (For example, a test case should not pause and prompt for a user input; all the information and additional resources that the test requires should be made available to the test at the time it is coded, or an automated mechanism should be developed to acquire such resources at run time.)

- Test case can be executed *independently of other test cases*. This requirement implies that there should be no dependency between the tests, and the tests should be able to run as if they are executed in isolation. (In particular, test cases should not produce side effects that may change the result of running other test cases.)[1]

■   Test cases are *units of organization and execution*. As units of organization, test cases are grouped into test suites.

Test Suite

A *test suite* is a collection of test cases or other test suites. The relationship between test cases and test suites is described by the Composite[2] pattern.

Test Fixture

A *test fixture* is a group of test cases sharing a common set of run-time resources.

Now that the concepts are defined, let's look at our test again:

```
using System;
using NUnit.Framework;


namespace NUnitQuickStart
{
    [TestFixture]
    public class NumbersFixture
    {
        [Test]
        public void AddTwoNumbers()
        {
            int a = 1;
            int b = 2;
            int sum = a + b;
            Assert.AreEqual(3, sum);
        }
    }
}
```

The second line (using NUnit.Framework;) references the NUnit namespace, which contains all the classes you need to use to write your programmer tests. Classes populating this namespace are packaged in *nunit.framework.dll*.

---

1. This requirement is an adaptation of the idea of *referential transparency*, which is borrowed from functional programming languages. A purely applicative program is completely devoid of any side effects, so it is much more conducive to mathematical verification of the program's correctness.

2. See *Design Patterns*.

Tests and Test Fixtures

One of the features of the NUnit Framework is its use of custom attributes. Attributes in .NET are the standard mechanisms to extend metadata about run-time entities. In this case, the run-time entities of interest are as follows:

- *Test classes* are the classes that contain test code; each test assembly has to have at lease one test class.

- *Test methods* are test cases; each test method represents a single test case that can be run independently of other test cases.

As the previous example demonstrates, the *[TestFixture]* attribute can be used to mark a class as a test class. The test class has to be public to be discovered by the test runner. The *[Test]* attribute is used to mark a method as a test method. A test method must follow these rules:

- The method must be declared as public.

- The method has to be an instance method (nonstatic).

- The return type is *void*.

- The method can't take any parameters.

Working with Test Runners

A *test runner* is a program that can be used to automatically discover, organize, run, and collect the results of execution of programmer tests. Until now, we have been working with NUnit-Gui test runner. One of the features of this test runner is its capability to represent the composite structure of the test assembly using a tree control, which provides a good visualization of the structure of the tests in the assembly. The test runner performs an automatic discovery of the tests in the assembly by following this simple two-step process:

1. Find all classes marked with the *[TestFixture]* attribute in the assembly.

2. For each fixture found, create a test suite and populate this test suite with all the test methods discovered in the test fixture.

After the test suite for the assembly is built, the test runner renders a visual representation of the test suite. In this tree, each non-leaf node maps to a test suite, and each leaf node maps to a test case. When the assembly is loaded, the tests can be run. You can run the entire suite or you might choose to run an individual node in the tree (a test suite or a test case) and run only that node and all its descendants. The test runner collects the results of the execution of each test case it runs and presents these results to you.

Assertions

A test case must be self-verifying. To write a self-verifying test case, we need a mechanism that supports such a verification process. In NUnit, the mechanism is called an *assertion*, which is a simple statement of truth (or what the programmer believes to be the truth). Here are some examples of assertions:

- 1 + 2 = 3. (In most number systems, this is so.)

- A dollar today is worth more than a dollar tomorrow. (If you disagree, we will be glad to hold your paychecks for you until you can figure out the one directly following.)

- $E = mc^2$

Assertions can be rather arbitrary and might lack mechanisms to support their verification. In NUnit, we decided to support the mechanisms to verify the first type of assertions.

In the example we wrote, we used the mechanism of assertions to verify the results of adding two numbers. Let's make a little change to this example. The only statement we will change is the following:

```
Assert.AreEqual(4,sum);
```

Obviously, this assumption will fail. To indicate failure, the progress bar turns red, and the tree nodes turn red to indicate which test failed. Note that the test tree represents a failure—the parent nodes are colored red if at least one child note is red (sibling nodes of a failing node are not affected by its failure). Figure A-5 demonstrates the NUnit-Gui window after we rerun the test:

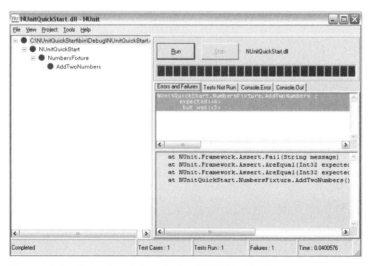

Figure A-5   Assertion failure in the NUnit-Gui test runner

This simple example demonstrates the role that assertions play in NUnit Framework. This role is twofold:

■ Assertions are the mechanism to implement the self-verification property of test cases.

■ Assertions are also used by test runners to collect and report failures.

Let's move on to a few more examples to demonstrate some other capabilities of NUnit.

Other NUnit Capabilities

With our previous example, we introduced the basic NUnit features and capabilities. *TestFixture*, *Test*, and *Assert* are the three most fundamental features that you need to know to start writing programmer tests with NUnit. What we will describe now will build on these three features.

Using SetUp/TearDown Attributes

In the definition of a test fixture that we gave earlier, we said that tests in a test fixture share a common set of run-time resources. These common run-time resources may need to be acquired and initialized in a certain way before a test is executed and released or cleaned up after the test is completed. NUnit supports this common initialization/cleanup process using two additional custom attributes: *SetUp* and *TearDown*. Let's extend the original example to demonstrate this capability. Let's add multiplication:

```
using System;
using NUnit.Framework;


namespace NUnitQuickStart
{
    [TestFixture]
    public class NumbersFixture
    {
        [Test]
        public void AddTwoNumbers()
        {
            int a = 1;
            int b = 2;
            int sum = a + b;
            Assert.AreEqual(3, sum);
        }
```

```
    [Test]
    public void MultiplyTwoNumbers()
    {
        int a = 1;
        int b = 2;
        int product = a * b;
        Assert.AreEqual(2, product);
    }
  }
}
```

We can share the initialization code of the operands by extracting this code into a separate method and marking this method with a *SetUp* attribute (the local variables have to change their scope and become instance variables). Here is the code after the change:

```
using System;
using NUnit.Framework;

namespace NUnitQuickStart
{
    [TestFixture]
    public class NumbersFixture
    {
        private int a;
        private int b;

        [SetUp]
        void InitializeOperands()
        {
            a = 1;
            b = 2;
        }

        [Test]
        public void AddTwoNumbers()
        {
            int sum = a + b;
            Assert.AreEqual(3, sum);
        }

        [Test]
        public void MultiplyTwoNumbers()
        {
            int product = a * b;
            Assert.AreEqual(2, product);
        }
    }
}
```

The NUnit test runner will execute the method marked with the *SetUp* attribute prior to each test.

Using *ExpectedException*

Now let's add division to the example. We want to make sure that dividing by zero works, as promised by the .NET documentation. Here is a test to verify this assumption.

```
[Test]
[ExpectedException(typeof(DivideByZeroException))]
public void DivideByZero()
{
    int zero = 0;
    int infinity = a/zero;
    Assert.Fail("Should have gotten an exception");
}
```

In addition to the *Test* attribute, the *DivideByZero* method has another custom attribute: *ExpectedException*. You can use this attribute to indicate that an exception of a particular type is expected during the execution of the test method. If the method completes without throwing the expected exception, the test fails. Using this attribute helps in writing programmer tests that verify boundary conditions.

Using the *Ignore* Attribute

Sometimes, we have tests that we don't want to run. There can be many reasons for this: you may be in the middle of a refactoring that is breaking a lot of tests and you can't stand the sight of the red bar; or you may have written a programmer test to capture some not-fully-understood requirements. Using the *Ignore* attribute, you can keep the tests but not execute them. Let's mark the *MultiplyTwoNumbers* test method with the *Ignore* attribute:

```
[Test]
[Ignore("Multiplication is ignored")]
public void MultiplyTwoNumbers()
{
    int product = a * b;
    Assert.AreEqual(2, product);
}
```

Running these tests now produces the following output (shown in Figure A-6):

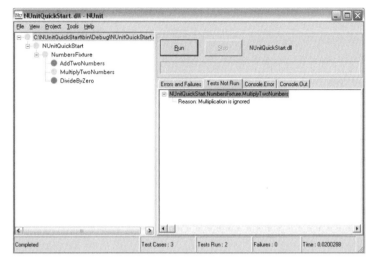

Figure A-6   Using the Ignore attribute with a programmer test

The *Ignore* attribute can be attached to either an individual test method or an entire test class (*TestFixture*). If the *Ignore* attribute is attached to the *Test-Fixture*, all the tests in the fixture will be ignored.

Using *TestFixtureSetUp/TestFixtureTearDown*

Sometimes, the resources needed by a set of tests are expensive to acquire. For example, database connections can be a critical resource, and opening/closing a database connection for every test in a test fixture may be too slow. NUnit has a pair of attributes that are similar to the *SetUp/TearDown* attributes discussed earlier: *TestFixtureSetUp/TestFixtureTearDown*. As their names suggest, these attributes are used to mark methods that initialize/release resources once for the entire test fixture.

For example, if we want to share the same database connection object for all the tests in our test fixture, we can write a method that opens a database connection and mark it with the *TestFixtureSetUp* attribute, another method that would close the database connection we would mark with the *TestFixtureTear-Down* attribute. Here is an example that demonstrates this:

```
using NUnit.Framework;

[TestFixture]
public class DatabaseFixture
{
   [TestFixtureSetUp]
   public void OpenConnection()
```

```
{
    //open the connection to the database
}

[TestFixtureTearDown]
public void CloseConnection()
{
    //close the connection to the database
}

[SetUp]
public void CreateDatabaseObjects()
{
    //insert the records into the database table
}

[TearDown]
public void DeleteDatabaseObjects()
{
    //remove the inserted records from the database table
}

[Test]
public void ReadOneObject()
{
    //load one record using the open database connection
}

[Test]
public void ReadManyObjects()
{
    //load many records using the open database connection
}

}
```

Test Life-Cycle Contract

If you recall our definition of the test case, one of the properties is the test's independence or isolation. The pair of *SetUp/TearDown* methods serves the purpose of achieving test isolation. *SetUp* makes sure that the shared resources are correctly initialized before each test is run, and *TearDown* makes sure that there are no leftover side effects produced by running tests. The *TestFixture-SetUp/TestFixtureTearDown* attributes serve a similar purpose, but at the test fixture scope. What we just described constitutes the *life-cycle contract* between the test framework's run-time container (test runner) and the tests you write.

To demonstrate this contract, we write a simple test that shows what methods get called and when. Here's the code:

```csharp
using System;
using NUnit.Framework;

[TestFixture]
public class LifeCycleContractFixture
{
   [TestFixtureSetUp]
   public void FixtureSetUp()
   {
      Console.Out.WriteLine("FixtureSetUp");
   }

   [TestFixtureTearDown]
   public void FixtureTearDown()
   {
      Console.Out.WriteLine("FixtureTearDown");
   }

   [SetUp]
   public void SetUp()
   {
      Console.Out.WriteLine("SetUp");
   }

   [TearDown]
   public void TearDown()
   {
      Console.Out.WriteLine("TearDown");
   }

   [Test]
   public void Test1()
   {
      Console.Out.WriteLine("Test 1");
   }

   [Test]
   public void Test2()
   {
      Console.Out.WriteLine("Test 2");
   }

}
```

When you compile and run this test, you see the following output in the console *System.Console* window:

```
FixtureSetUp
SetUp
Test 1
TearDown
SetUp
Test 2
TearDown
FixtureTearDown
```

As you can see, the *SetUp/TearDown* methods are called before and after each test method; the *TestFixtureSetUp/TestFixtureTearDown* methods are called once for the entire fixture.

Using the Visual Studio .NET Debugger with NUnit-Gui

As you write more and more programmer tests, you might spend less time debugging your application. Small and isolated programmer tests usually do a very good job of narrowing down bugs to a few lines of code. However, sometimes you might need to use a debugger to locate a particularly slippery bug. Let's say you have a failing programmer test, but you cannot identify the problem by simply looking at the code. Fortunately, using the Visual Studio .NET Debugger with NUnit-Gui is very straightforward.

First, you need to set up NUnit-Gui as your test runner with Visual Studio .NET (this process was described earlier). Second, you need to set a break point in the failing programmer test code and start the application in the Debug mode. Let's demonstrate this with our *NumberFixture* class. We will make a change to the *AddTwoNumbers* method to make it fail:

```
[Test]
public void AddTwoNumbers()
{
   int sum = a + b;
   Assert.AreEqual(4, sum);
}
```

We changed the expected value from 3 to 4, and the test now fails. Now we can set up a break point in the *AddTwoNumbers* method and start the Debug session. NUnit-Gui will appear and we will hit the Run button. When the execution reaches the *AddTwoNumbers* test, the Debugger will stop at the break point. Figure A-7 demonstrates this state:

Figure A-7 Using Visual Studio .NET Debugger with the NUnit-Gui test runner

Now we can debug the application as usual. The problem with the code is fairly obvious.

Appendix B

Transactions in ADO.NET

ADO.NET has built-in support for transactions, and transactional support in ADO.NET can be roughly divided into two categories: transaction management and transaction participation. Transaction management application programming interfaces (APIs) give ADO.NET applications a mechanism to explicitly manage transaction demarcation boundaries. Transaction participation allows transaction-aware resources to be enlisted with a transaction managed by some other entity—such as an external Transaction Manager.

Transaction Management

There are two main approaches to transaction management in enterprise applications:

- Manual or explicit transaction management
- Automatic or declarative transaction management

With manual transaction management, the application's code has explicit statements to start and terminate the transaction. Although transactional boundaries are fixed, an application has fine-grained control over how the transaction is managed. The application is responsible for the coordination of exception handling and transaction termination; for example, if some application code throws an exception, the enclosing transaction often needs to be manually rolled back.

Automatic transaction management relies on a Transaction Management Service to handle most of the transaction demarcation logic. A Transaction Management Service determines the rules that govern the way an application's code participates in transaction demarcation. The application code that uses automatic transaction management has to indicate when to start and terminate the transaction to the external Transaction Manager.

Manual Transaction Management

The *IDbConnection* and *IDbTransaction* interfaces are at the lowest level of the ADO.NET API we have. They can be used to manually manage database transactions. The *IDbCommand* interface has a *Transaction* property that can be set to associate the command with the specified transaction. All the commands enlisted with a transaction will be executed within that transaction's context; all the commands enlisted with a transaction will either commit or be rolled back as one unit of work. If the transaction is rolled back, all changes made by all the commands associated with the transaction will be undone in the database. Here is a sample to demonstrate the flow:

```
private static void RunATransaction()
{
    IDbConnection connection = GetConnection();
    IDbTransaction transaction = null;
    try
    {
        connection.Open();
        transaction = connection.BeginTransaction();

        IDbCommand command1 = …;
        command1.Transaction = transaction;

        IDbCommand command2 = …;
        command2.Transaction = transaction;

        command1.ExecuteNonQuery();
        command2.ExecuteNonQuery();

        transaction.Commit();
    }
    catch(Exception)
    {
        transaction.Rollback();
    }
    finally
    {
        connection.Close();
    }
}
```

This example demonstrates the manual transaction management capabilities of the ADO.NET framework. The control flow follows the same pattern:

■ Begin a transaction (*connection.BeginTransaction()*).

- Associate all the transactional resources with the transaction (*command1.Transaction = transaction*).

- Perform an interaction with a transaction-capable data source using the transactional resources associated with the Transaction Manager (*command1.ExecuteNonQuery()*).

- Handle application exceptions; if necessary, manage the rollback of the transaction (*transaction.Rollback()*).

- Release the transactional resources (*connection.Close()*).

In the example shown previously, all the transaction management is done within one method: *RunATransaction*. (The transaction is started, executed, and committed or rolled back within the boundaries of this one method.) With manual transaction management, you are not required to confine the transaction to one method; you can write code where a transaction spans multiple method invocations.

Automatic Transaction Management

ADO.NET also supports automatic transaction management, which relies on the mechanism of associating the caller's thread with a transaction. Instances of *IDbConnection* can be pooled, and the pool manager can be integrated with the external Transaction Manager. When an application issues a request to open a connection, the external Transaction Manager determines whether there is an existing transaction associated with the thread of the caller; if there is one, the connection returned to the caller will also be associated with this transaction.

Not all classes that use the ADO.NET API will automatically participate in automatic transaction management. Transaction management is one of the enterprise services available to specially developed components; some other services include just-in-time activation, security, object pooling, queued components, synchronization, and so on.

Application code has to be written and packaged in a specific way to take advantage of these enterprise services. For example, the application components have to be packaged in a strongly named assembly and registered with the COM+ run time. Application classes that are authored to meet these requirements are called serviced components; these classes use attributes to describe the services that they require and service-specific configuration information. Here is a code fragment to demonstrate a serviced component that uses automatic transaction management service:

```
[Transaction(TransactionOption.Required)]
public class Account : ServicedComponent
```

```
    {
        [AutoCommit(true)]
        public void Deposit(decimal amount)
        {}
}
```

The application class has to extend the *ServicedComponent* class; this is required of all serviced components. The *Account* class has a class-level attribute: *[Transaction(TransactionOption.Required)]*. This attribute indicates that the class requires the automatic transaction management service, and the value of the attribute *TransactionOption.Required* states that all access to the services of this class must be made within a transactional context.

When the thread of control enters this component, the Transaction Manager will determine whether there is a transaction associated with this thread. If there is one, the *Account* component will automatically be associated with the existing transaction; if there is no transaction in progress, the Transaction Manager will start a new one and associate it with the thread of control. Several other values for the Transaction attribute allow the application developer to choose the desired behavior:

- *Disabled*

- *NotSupported*

- *RequiresNew*

- *Supported*

The other aspect of interaction of the transaction-aware serviced component with the Transaction Manager is in the transaction termination logic. In the preceding example code, the *[AutoCommit(true)]* attribute is associated with the *Deposit* method of our *Account* component. This attribute tells the Transaction Manager to automatically commit the transaction started on behalf of this component if the method executes without throwing an exception. If an exception occurs, the Transaction Manager will automatically roll back the transaction. The other option is to explicitly vote for transaction rollback or commit using the *SetAbort* and *SetCommit* methods of the *ContextUtil* class.

Transaction Participation

Transaction-aware resources might be enlisted in a transaction. An example of a transaction-aware resource in ADO.NET is a Command object, which has a reference to a Connection object and can be configured to participate in a transaction by setting its *Transaction* property. When a command is enlisted in a transaction, it executes its database access logic as part of the contained transaction. Such transactional participation allows commands to see the changes of other commands participating in the same transaction before the transaction is completed; it also allows related commands to run as one unit of work and coordinate their changes to assure the consistent state of the system.

Appendix C

Bibliography

Alur, Deepak, John Crupi, and Dan Malks. *Core J2EE Patterns: Best Practices and Design Strategies.* Upper Saddle River, NJ: Prentice Hall, 2003.

Astels, David. *Test-Driven Development: A Practical Guide.* Upper Saddle River, NJ: Prentice Hall, 2003.

Ballinger, Keith. *.NET Web Services: Architecture and Implementation in .NET.* Boston: Addison-Wesley, 2003.

Beck, Kent. *Extreme Programming Explained: Embrace Change.* The XP Series. Boston: Addison-Wesley, 2000.

———. *Test-Driven Development: By Example.* Boston: Addison-Wesley, 2003.

Binder, Robert. *Testing Object-Oriented Systems: Models, Patterns, and Tools.* Boston: Addison-Wesley, 1999.

Box, Don, Aaron Skonnard, and John Lam. *Essential XML.* Boston: Addison-Wesley, 2000.

Cockburn, Alistair. *Agile Software Development.* Boston: Addison-Wesley, 2001.

Evans, Eric. *Domain-Driven Design: Tackling Complexity in the Heart of Software.* Boston: Addison-Wesley, 2003.

Feathers, Michael. *The Humble Dialog Box. http://www.objectmentor.com/resources /articles,* 2002.

Fowler, Martin. *Patterns of Enterprise Application Architecture.* Boston: Addison-Wesley, 2003.

———. *The Refactoring Home Page. http://www.refactoring.com.*

———. *Refactoring: Improving the Design of Existing Code.* Boston: Addison-Wesley, 1999.

———. *UML Distilled: A Brief Guide to the Standard Object Modeling Language.* 3rd ed. Boston: Addison-Wesley, 2003.

Gamma, Erich, and Kent Beck. *JUnit: A Cook's Tour.* Java Report. *http://junit.source-forge.net/doc/cookstour/cookstour.htm,* May 1999.

Gamma, Erich, Richard Helm, Ralph Johnson, and John Vlissides. *Design Patterns: Elements of Reusable Object-Oriented Software.* Boston: Addison-Wesley, 1994.

Hohpe, Gregor, and Bobby Woolf. *Enterprise Integration Patterns*. Boston: Addison-Wesley, 2003.

Hunt, Andrew, and David Thomas. *The Pragmatic Programmer*. Boston: Addison-Wesley, 2000.

Jeffries, Ron. *Extreme Programming Adventures in C#*. Redmond, WA: Microsoft Press, 2004.

Jeffries, Ron, Ann Anderson, and Chet Hendrickson. *Extreme Programming Installed*. The XP Series. Boston: Addison-Wesley, 2001.

Link, Johannes. *Unit Testing in Java: How Tests Drive the Code*. San Francisco: Morgan Kaufmann, 2003.

Marick, Brian. *The Craft of Software Testing*. Upper Saddle River, NJ: Prentice Hall, 1995.

———. *Testing Foundations Home Page. http://www.testing.com*.

Martin, Robert C., James Newkirk, and Robert Koss. *Agile Software Development: Principles, Patterns and Practices*. Upper Saddle River, NJ: Prentice Hall, 2003.

Massol, Vincent. *JUnit in Action*. Greenwich, CT: Manning Publications, 2004.

McBreen, Pete. *Software Craftsmanship*. Boston: Addison-Wesley, 2002.

Meyer, Bertrand. *Object-Oriented Software Construction*. 2nd ed. Upper Saddle River, NJ: Prentice Hall, 1988.

Microsoft Corporation. *Enterprise Solution Patterns in .NET*. Microsoft Patterns & Practices, *http://www.microsoft.com/resources/practices/*, 2003.

Newkirk, James, and Robert C. Martin. *Extreme Programming in Practice*. The XP Series. Boston: Addison-Wesley, 2001.

Richter, Jeffrey. *Applied Microsoft .NET Framework Programming*. Redmond, WA: Microsoft Press, 2002.

Short, Scott. *Building XML Web Services for the Microsoft .NET Platform*. Redmond, WA: Microsoft Press, 2002.

Skonnard, Aaron, and Martin Gudgin. *Essential XML Quick Reference*. Boston: Addison-Wesley, 2001.

Tate, Bruce. *Bitter Java*. Greenwich, CT: Manning Publications, 2002.

Wake, William. *Extreme Programming Explored*. The XP Series. Boston: Addison-Wesley, 2001.

———. *Refactoring Workbook*. Boston: Addison-Wesley, 2003.

Wells, Don and Laurie Williams, eds. *Extreme Programming and Agile Method—XP/Agile Universe 2002*. New York: Springer-Verlag, 2002.

Wildermuth, Shawn. *Pragmatic ADO.NET: Data Access for the Internet World*. Boston: Addison-Wesley, 2003.

Index

S

About the Authors

James Newkirk is the development lead for the Microsoft Platform Architecture Guidance team, building guidance and reusable assets for enterprise customers through the Patterns & Practices series. Prior to joining Microsoft, he coauthored *Enterprise Solution Patterns in .NET* (Microsoft Press) and *Extreme Programming in Practice* (Addison-Wesley). In between writing books and consulting on software projects, James led the development of NUnit V2. He can be reached at *jamesnew@microsoft.com*.

Alexei A. Vorontsov has been a software developer for more than eight years. He has developed software in a variety of environments, from scientific mathematical applications to enterprise systems. His interests include development, testing, and management of large distributed software solutions and pragmatic application of agile methods to meet the goals of enterprise system development in a cost-efficient manner.